Writing it Right

Writing it Right

To invite the authors to speak
or lead a Writing It Right workshop,
contact Coleen at www.coleenparatore.com

Peg Spain Murtagh
& Coleen Paratore

While the incidents in this book did happen, some of the names and personal characteristics of some of the individuals have been changed. Any resulting resemblance to persons living or dead is entirely coincidental and unintentional.

Cover design by The Troy Book Makers
Book design by Jessika Hazelton

Printed in the United States of America

The Troy Book Makers • Troy, New York • thetroybookmakers.com

To order additional copies of this title,
contact your favorite local bookstore
or visit www.tbmbooks.com

ISBN: 978-1-61468-244-8

To my daughter Coleen
who shared herself and her writer's gifts with me
which enabled me to unlock my heart and reveal myself.

Col, without your unwavering love and endless encouragement
this work of mine would have remained unwritten.

— psm

⁂

To my mother, Peg Spain Murtagh,
always my greatest teacher,

To my sons, Dylan, Connor, and Christopher Paratore,
forever my greatest joys,

To you reading these words right now,
pour out pain, plant seeds, and
write yourself right who you want to be.

— Coleen Murtagh Paratore

"Reading books changes lives.
So does writing them."

— Sarah Ban Breathnach
Simple Abundance

Contents

Winter

Spring

Summer

Fall

Dear Reader,

Welcome.

We hope our book will make a happy difference in your life – be a friend to lean on as you journey through a challenging time, seek to connect with others on a deeper level, or gather the confidence to chart a new course.

Perhaps you will use the topics herein as kindling for conversations or book club discussions, or as spark-starters for writing what *only you* can write.

May you find enjoyment, peace, and inspiration in these pages.

With love and gratitude,
Coleen and *Peggy*
September 2014

Our Beginning

(as told by Coleen)

I conceived of this book as a way of keeping my mother alive.

It was Thanksgiving morning 2012 and I was jogging through Frear Park near my home in Troy, New York, ruminating about the shopping craze of Black Friday becoming "Gray Thursday" this year and how the real things in life to be thankful for are not things you buy, and how it was my mother who taught me that, my wise and wonderful mother now again in the throes of severe depression, the worst it has ever been.

As I ran past Conway Court apartments where she lives, an idea sparked: *Mom and I should write a book together* – about the things we are thankful for. In my novel *Sunny Holiday,* 9-year-old Sunny and her Mom are writing a book like that called "Free All Year." They plan to get it published and "meet Oprah." ***Mom and I should do that.***

After decades of valiant effort battling a host of troubles, my mother seems to have lost the strength to fight. I fear she is giving up. I refuse to let her go.

My mother, Peg Spain Murtagh, will be 75 in January. So far she has survived a traumatic estrangement from her own mother at the age of 15 and not seeing her again for 28 years; the deaths of two infant sons; three miscarriages; divorce; the raising of six children while also working outside the home; a horrific car accident; a life-long battle with obesity; two heart attacks; two open heart surgeries; a devastating Christmas fire; COPD; the installation of a pace-maker; atrial fibrillation; and now greatly slowed mobility -- and yet those myriad challenges pale in comparison to the debilitating, chronic depression which, despite counseling, medications, and in-patient programs offering patches of peace, *viciously returns* -- a doomsday reaper of despair making simple tasks like getting out of bed or taking a shower seem impossible.

Twice in the past, when her depression was darkest, my mother attempted suicide. I am afraid that she is falling toward that grave outlet again. I will not let that happen.

Perhaps *writing*....writing a book together...might be the answer.

My mother loves to write. She always seems most engaged, *alive*, when writing. Could this book be a big enough happy goal...something worth living for?

A few days after Thanksgiving, I ran the idea by my mother.

"Oh, Col, no," she said. "I'm in such a bad place."

"We'll keep it simple, Mom, a page a week, a few sentences. It will be fun."

"No." She looked hopeless.

"It would help me, too, Mom." My mother more than anyone knows I am still grieving the end of my 28-year marriage. It's been nearly five years and I am in a happy relationship with a wonderful new man, Columbus, yet I still haven't moved on.

"We might help others, too," I said. "We could spark a writing club trend, people helping people move forward. Maybe we'll even meet Oprah."

Mom attempted a smile.

Finally, after a long catalog of woes why this wouldn't work, she began talking about writers who inspire her.

"I have Pema Chodron (Buddhist nun) in my pocketbook right now," she said. "Reading Pema always makes me feel better."

"Great," I said. "One day people will say, 'I've got Peg Murtagh in my pocket right now.'"

My mother laughed, such a lovely thing to see.

"Okay, Col. I'll give it a try."

And so we're off.

Who knows where this will lead.

That's half the fun of it.

For me with writing, the *surprise* is always the best part.

-Coleen Murtagh Paratore, December 3, 2012

Winter

Week 1, December 4, 2012

Poetry – Free-Writing

We met for tea at 3:00 pm at Mom's apartment during a snowstorm. There was classical music playing. On the small table by the window, she'd set out steaming mugs of green tea and a centerpiece consisting of two miniature candy canes and *one* foil-wrapped Hershey kiss. There were pink cocktail napkins with the quote:

"I don't know much about being a millionaire,
but I bet I'd be darling at it."

Dorothy Parker

We laughed about that.

"How are you doing, Mom?" I asked.

"Not good at all." She elaborated and I listened.

"Why don't you read first," I suggested.

"I'm a poet, Col. In my heart of hearts that's what I am." Then she shared this:

psm, 12-4-12

Let me speak my poetry
the language of my heart
What else is there
after 75 years
(must you rhyme with tears? or fears?)
Why not cheers?
It takes a poem
to put words to music
to make a song
it doesn't take long
Where is my strength

would I go to any length
Without a song
without a poem
I cannot fashion myself
or even know myself
Perhaps on these pages
I can share my poetry with you
It's what I do
It is my love song
to each one of you
Thank you.

⁂

"I love this, Mom," I said. "It reminds me of Emily Dickinson."

"She's my favorite poet," my mother said, opening notebooks to show me poems she'd written at various happy and sad moments throughout her life. She then reached for another notebook. This one outlined wishes for her memorial service someday.

"Well we won't need this for a *very long time*," I said, "but I'm glad to know what you're thinking." The exchange was not sad, rather peaceful and easy.

"I want this poem by Emily Dickinson on my prayer card," Mom said, then read:

If I can stop one heart from breaking,
I shall not live in vain;
If I can ease one life the aching,
Or cool one pain,
Or help one fainting robin
Unto his nest again,
I shall not live in vain.

I held back tears. We looked over Mom's poem again.

"Do you think I need the 'thank you' at the end?" she asked.

"I like it," I said. "It's perfect." We talked some more, then I read:

cmp, 12-4-12

"Free Writing"

In my teens on the night I was molested and nearly raped...in my twenties when my best friend died...in my thirties when I lost my first baby...in my forties when my mother attempted suicide...in my fifties when my divorce became final...at those times and on countless other less traumatic yet equally difficult days....I wrote about how I was feeling until I felt strong enough to go on.

The single best way I know how to make my way out of darkness into light is to write. Pen on paper, I pour out the pain until I can plant some seeds of hope.

Long before I learned writing scholar Peter Elbow's term "free writing" in a graduate course on writing at Trinity College in Hartford, Connecticut, pursuing my master's degree in English Literature in the 1980s, I was free writing about my feelings in a floral-covered journal with a blue Bic pen, late at night in bed as a child.

To me, free writing is writing what I'm *hearing within,* without a plan, as fast as I can, cracking open a vein, ink on paper, letting the inside out....and when I'm finished....ahhh....I am lighter for the letting go.

I have written myself "right" again.

⁂ ⁂ ⁂

"I love this, Col," my mother said, "really."

She started reading it over again with her "editor face" on.

I smiled, unwrapped the one Hershey kiss, and popped it into my mouth. Here, despite all the books I've had published, my Mom still critiques my work the way she did at that gray and white speckled Formica table with the wobbly leg propped up with a folded Christmas card in our kitchen at 16th High Street when I was Sunny Holiday's age.

⁂ ⁂ ⁂ ⁂ ⁂

Week 2, December 11, 2012

Music – Wise Words

We met for lunch at the Country View Diner on Hoosick Road. My mother asked for "a booth by the window," always our preference, and the host obliged.

"Did you write something, Mom?" I asked.

"Yes," she said, not smiling, "but I'm only doing this because you asked me to."

Her soup arrived as she began reading, so I offered to read it aloud instead:

psm, 12-11-12

"No Music No Me"

There has not ever been a time, past or present, when music has not been part of me. Simply, it's just part of what defines me. Always will be.

In one early music memory, back in the 40s, I was 6 or 7, we were living in the upstairs flat at 1600 Hutton Street in Beman Park and I was taking piano lessons. To get to my teacher's house, I would walk alone, across a field (later owned by RPI), then up a steep hill, then across Burdett Avenue to a side street.

My piano teacher's name has always stayed with me – Avila LaPlante. (There's a panic part in that memory; only a small part, but at the time it was big. I was walking back from my lesson and as I crossed that long field I was suddenly confronted by a large dog, bounding right at me. His two front paws were right up at my shoulders, his panting face in my face. Someone in a house nearby heard my screams, called the dog, and I was saved. That's just an aside to my music remembrances, but a remembrance of panic just the same and it always comes to mind when I think of my childhood days and piano lessons.)

The bigger, happier music remembrance from that same time is this:

Miss LaPlante taught her students so well that we got to perform at Troy Music Hall. Imagine me, barely 8, all dressed up in a beautiful long empire style gown, getting to be in a recital in that world famous place. I don't remember my solo, but I do remember being up on that stage, bowing proudly to my audience.

Music, always music. Still in the 1940s, during World War II, my sisters Janie and Virginia and I sang for anyone who would listen – a hit from the big band era, "Three Little Sisters." (Any senior body remember The Andrew Sisters?)

> *"One loved a soldier,*
> *one loved a sailor,*
> *and one loved a lad from the Marines"*

Janie and I walked around our Beman Park neighborhood singing as part of our wartime "Good Neighbor Policy."

After the war, music followed me again when our family moved down to 3 Eagle Street, from St. Paul's to St. Peter's parish. More piano lessons ensued, now from the sisters in the rectory at the academy. I don't remember those lessons taking me far, but I certainly loved being in the choir and later getting to stay up like a grown-up for Midnight Mass in 7th and 8th grade, singing those beautiful Gregorian chants.

When I got to Catholic High, I tried out for the Freshman Talent Show and made the audition. I sang "Blue Moon." I also sang for the Spanish Club. I still remember some of the Spanish lyrics for "Day After Day I'll Always Love You." (don't check my spelling), but something like:

> *"Yah hay amor querida mia, lindo amor querida mia, suenos,*
> *ya lucen en mi ojos, besos, me dan at frenesi..."*

Some high school students in the fifties had their own bands and played at "sock hops" around town. In one band, one of the best drummers, Don Marincelli, asked me to be his vocalist. I was thrilled, so I asked my father's permission, to which he responded in so many words, "Over my dead body."

So went my not-to-be music career.

All through the fifties I sang along with Patti Page, Pat Boone, Johnny Ray ("*If your sweetheart sends a letter of goodbye, it's no secret you'll feel better if you cry.*"), Elvis Presley ("Are You Lonesome Tonight?"), and so many others. The top forty on vinyl 45s or 78s played on every radio station.

The thing with me and my music is the music has been with me through all the good times and all the not-so-good times. At some point, I guess in the early fifties, our family acquired an old piano, a gift from the family of a deceased elderly Spain relative who lived not far from us. The story goes that the piano was rolled over Ninth Street on casters and took up residence in our living room. I don't remember playing it much although I'm sure my sister, Janie, and I did.

What I do remember is sitting next to my mother on the piano bench which was big enough for two. My mother is fingering with one hand, "*You Always Hurt the One You Love.*" Whenever I hear that old song, I remember my mother and the song she chose, and me and the old piano.

(Col's note: Overcome with emotion, I stopped reading here. I never met my grandmother. The thought of my mother sitting next to *her mother*, side by side on a piano bench, happily making music together was just so painfully beautiful.)

So give me any decade from the 40s on, give me a song and I'll sing it all or whatever I can remember of it. Another favorite of mine is Patsy Cline singing "*Crazy.*"

What a loss. And so many Johnny Cash favorites. His music gifts go on.

As recently as my 70th birthday celebration, I sang and danced the golden oldies thanks to my children who arranged for a deejay to bring all my favorites.

Right up to my present, right now, 2012, my 18-year-old grandson Dylan finds in the palm of his hand with his 21st century technology, like magic, the Mills Brothers, and they are singing for me: "*Up a lazy river by the old mill run, the lazy lazy river in the noon day sun...*"

And right to this minute as I end this writing, an old song lingers in my heart and speaks my truth, which has been my truth forever, and it goes something like this:

Without a song, the day would never end;
Without a song, the road would never bend;
Without a song, I haven't got a friend;
Without a song.

* * *

"Here you go again, Mom," I said, wiping away tears. "You say you have nothing good to say and then, oh my God, look what you write! This is beautiful."

I recalled how on Thanksgiving we were sitting around the table at my sister Noreen's house playing games when all of a sudden, my mother started singing. My brother, Jerry, took out his pocket recorder. Nor held up her phone to tape. We sat riveted as my Mom sang.... *Blue Moon* and *Chattanooga Choo-Choo* and *Are You Lonesome Tonight* like she was on a stage. She sang so well she could have been.

I took out my piece and read:

cmp, 12-11-12

Wise Words

Running in the rain this morning, all my worries tagged along. How will my sons, Chris, Connor, and Dylan, react when I tell them Columbus is moving in with me? When will I get a new contract? Money is tight. I need to sell my Cape house, but it will break my heart…on and on I worried, then heard this inside: "*Let life lead you.*"

Years ago, I was stressing with worries and my dear friend, Kathy Johnson, said, "You can't keep trying to control everything. You'll drive yourself crazy or make yourself sick. Why don't you try letting life *lead you* for a change?"

What a novel idea: *let life lead.* Maybe I don't have to plan it all, manage it all, for all to be well. In fact, perhaps all would be "weller" if I stepped aside and *let life lead.*

"Life" being God...Love...Spirit...Good...all one and the same to me.

* * * * *

Week 3, December 20, 2012

Giving – Grandchildren

I drove to Mom's for tea at 3:00 pm. She'd been sick in bed with a stomach virus and was "*really* down" with her depression, but reluctantly agreed to still meet.

On the table by the window were mugs of orange, passion fruit and jasmine green tea, and Fig Newton cookies, two for each of us. I read first:

cmp, 12-20-12

"Some Kinda Gift"

In these days leading up to Christmas, and as our nation reels from the horrific massacre of 20 children and 6 teachers at the Sandy Hook Elementary School in Newtown Connecticut, I keep thinking about how I can get out of myself and *give more.*

One cold winter day, many years ago -- I was six or so -- I was hurrying home after school when I saw my Mom sitting on our front steps talking to a shabbily dressed stranger. My Nana would have called him a hobo; today we'd say homeless. I watched fascinated as my mother listened to the man, nodding her head with interest, smiling.

I don't remember discussing this scene with my Mom at the time, but decades later when she became Director of Joseph's House, a homeless shelter in Troy, and created the "Winter Walk for the Homeless," (although my ever-humble mother never takes credit), I recalled that cold day long ago and how she'd given that stranger a true gift. She looked him in the eyes and smiled, let him know he mattered, that someone cared enough to *listen to his story*.

My mother has lived a life of service to others. Not sitting on boards of directors or writing thousand-dollar checks, although those, too, are worthy philanthropic efforts, my Mom was the one quietly delivering meals, taking her AIDS care-team buddy, John, to his Baptist church on Sunday, teaching adults to read…

When I became a mother, with Chris in 1989, then Connor in 1992, finally Dylan, in 1994, it was important to me to instill in them the notion of giving back. They may recall how we supported a young boy from Thailand, Bobby Sumbotum, paying for his meals, lodging, and schooling; or perhaps the summer 8-yr-old Niko from the Bronx, who didn't know how to swim or ride a bike, spent two weeks with us; or the Christmas we helped an Albany family, delivering clothes and toys to their grim apartment, a *Tale of Two Cities* away from our balsam-wreath-on-the-door brick colonial in suburbia.

As much as my ex-husband Tony and I gave throughout all of our sons' growing up years, I felt certain we should do more. Tony used to joke that I'd "give all our money away," and yet he was always equally generous, contributing to the American Cancer Society and Heart Association among other causes.

Two years ago, Connor, Chris, Dylan, and I delivered $500 worth of new books for the children in low-income housing sponsored by the YWCA of the Greater Capital Region where I serve on the Board. I felt so proud as my three handsome sons carried in those boxes. Last year, I "adopted" a woman through the Y's Holiday Appeal, buying everything on her wish list, dishes, silverware, linens, etc, then added some fun stuff too. I bought presents to make up five "holiday gift bags" for some Y women. Dylan, and his friend, Cameron, (Columbus' son) wrapped the gifts at our kitchen table.

In my Willa books, I invested Willa with the belief that we each owe "community rent" – a portion of our time, talent, or treasure – to help make a difference in the world. In *The Cupid Chronicles*, Willa helps save her town library. In *Willa by Heart,* she inspires an affordable housing initiative. In *Wish I Might,* she creates "Change for Good" jars for charity. (Willa is like a daughter. I do pray I get to write more Willa books!)

This holiday season my budget was tight, but I still made up 5 gift bags for Y women. Dylan helped wrap the journals, 2013 planning calendars, decks of cards, notepads, pens, scented hand lotion, bubble bath, Cherry Cordials, Peanut Brittle, a Bingo Game, *Chicken Soup for the Mother's Soul*, photo frames, pocket photo albums, gently worn scarves, boxes of jewelry, and signed copies of one of my books. When we delivered the bags, a YW staff person offered us a banana. Dyl and I each took one. It was a nice exchange. "That was a good thing, Mom," Dyl said.

The Park Pub down the street from me is a warm friendly place like *Cheers* where everyone knows your name. Each December the Pub staff sets up a "giving tree" with tags listing requests from local children in need. This year I chose this one:

12 year old boy: likes to sing wants "**some kinda gift**"

Columbus, a fine singer in his own right, said "don't worry, Luv, I've got this."

He combed through the Sunday store fliers and found a "versatile MP3 player" with FM radio, video, touch screen, that you can download music and photos on for $30.

"He's going to love this," Columbus said, wrapping the gift.

"We're a good team," I said.

* * *

"That's just beautiful, Col," my mother said.

"Tell me more about your community service work," I asked.

Mom smiled recalling times with her "AIDS buddy, John," part of a care team from Christ Sun of Justice parish, based at RPI. "I took John to the Latham Diner once and he ordered prime rib... *prime rib*. I wasn't sure how I would pay for it." She laughed. "And then there was Jean Holstein. She was the widow of the deacon at my church. She suffered from MS that over time rendered her completely immobile, crippled from the neck down. I brought Jean communion every week and we'd talk."

"How long did you do that for, Mom?"

"A few years," she said. "It was really *being with* someone." She locked eyes with me. "These aren't nice things you do, Col -- these are *gifts that you are given.*"

And then my mother read:

psm, 12-20-12

Oh the Children of My Children

Here we go; she's going to start bragging about her grandchildren. Ho hum.

The truth is – one by one these eight precious beings have taken up residence in my heart beginning with Chris (9-4-89); and here in my heart they remain at the end of 2012.

In chronological order after Chris, they are his brother Connor (10-10-92), then Nor and Mike's Ryan (3-12-94), back to Col and Tony's Dylan (7-6-94). Next, Kevin and his wife, Colleen's, first born Liam (10-8-98), then Ry's brother Jack (3-6-00). Kev and Coll's one and only daughter and my one and only granddaughter, Lauren (5-21-01), and finally Kev and Coll's Brendan (10-01-03).

All the clichés grandparents voice when bragging about their grandchildren come to mind and it's the clichés I struggle to avoid. These beautiful human beings deserve so much more and better than I can pen. But in this writing effort I'm remembering with my daughter, Coleen, the positives in my life, so I'll share just a bit of the bliss I know. It's impossible to encapsulate 23 years of grandmother joy in a page or two. And, of course, (you'll have to trust me because it's true), they are all beautiful, talented, and close (very close) to brilliant.

My first grandchild, **Christopher**, gave me my grandma name which is "Tama." Tama is a combination of Grandma and Tara (my cat at the time). Chris said it first. His Mom, my daughter, Coleen, had brought him for a visit. When they were leaving, he was told, "Say goodbye to Grandma; say goodbye to Tara." Chris was just a toddler and meant to say "Bye, Tara, bye Grandma," but it came out "Bye Tara, bye Tama," and that's how I became Tama to all of my grandchildren. It never occurred to me, or to Coleen, to correct this beautiful child, who already at that young age had a way with words. Maybe it runs in the family. Thank heaven.

Connor, now in college, always makes me smile. His beautiful eyes draw me toward what I can only describe as Connor's inner wonder.

Dylan, (my Dilly Bo Billy), who honored me when he asked me to be his Godmother now some ten years ago, and so has given me one treasure upon another.

Ryan, so talented, now in college, always reminds me of his growing up years in White Plains, NY, when at Christmas, barely two, dressed in a tuxedo, he entertained us singing, dancing with, excuse me, a mike. He couldn't have been happier, nor could he have made us any happier.

And his brother **Jack**, now growing up so bright, way beyond his years, winner of so many awards as he moves toward middle school; and making his mark not only on the basketball court, but his Mom's student in theatre, performing in Brewster in stand-up comedy and improv.

And **Liam**, this son of Saint Patrick I spoke of in poetry at his Mom and Dad's wedding day, has only gotten more handsome, excelling in his high school studies, and couldn't be a nicer young man, so polite, thoughtful, a pleasure to be with.

And my beautiful **Lauren** who gives so much joy just watching her grow up. I can see her as a wee one, already standing on a big chair at the kitchen sink washing the tea party dishes, so secure in her task. And she has never stopped. She helps her Mom today and every day. If you know what a working Mom does when she gets home, that's what Lauren does. A darling girl is Lauren, showing me what a strong, courageous, powerful and feminine woman-to-be looks like.

And my youngest grandchild, **Brendan**, who is growing to be his own self – handsome, smart, great at sports, and a champion of the down and out, who is always willing to help someone in need. And, like all of my grandchildren, always ready for a game of Canasta with Tama.

Eight grandchildren. Twenty-three years of bliss. Whatever have I done to deserve this? The answer I tell myself, of course, is this: Nothing. You've done nothing. A great God has so loved you, so say "thank you." Say it every day in every way by honoring the gift of your own life.

On a light note, here's some good counsel hanging on my bedroom wall:

Grandchildren are the reward you get for not strangling your teenagers.

Week 4, December 27, 2012

Meditation – Rainbows

I drove to Mom's for tea at 3:00 pm. Hanging on her apartment door was the familiar carved wooden peace dove and inside there was holiday music playing, but for the first time, no ceramic table-top Christmas tree, no angel chimes hanging from the ceiling.

The place looked uncluttered, boxes stacked about. Mom has been quietly giving away her few material possessions --books, photographs, decorative items, etc.

We sat at the little table by the window. It was snowing.

Mom served our now favorite green tea with orange, passion fruit and jasmine, and pointed to some cookies. "They're hard, but if you dunk them in tea they're fine."

Laughing, I tested out the theory.

"I wrote about meditation on Christmas," Mom said, then read:

psm, 12-27-12

Be Still and Hear Me

There's a wonder to be known
If I can only sit alone

It's the Word of God
Be still
Call it what you will

In the quiet moment
In the opening of day
I am called to remember and pray

Don't go away – please stay
I have something to say

I sit and breathe and receive
The gift within

In silence I listen
And hear a plea
God asking something that will be
Please sit and watch one hour with me

And then I hear the gift
The silent voice of God
It fills my being
With Symphony

I come to know the miracle
The presence always there
All my gifts I now have heard
All hearing is all knowing
In the Silence of the Word

⁂

"That's amazing, Mom."

"Thanks, Col." She shook her head sadly. "This isn't easy for me. I couldn't even get myself up off the couch yesterday."

"I know, Mom, but your writing is such a gift and I think God expects you to..."

My mother laughed. She knew where I was going with this. "Just offer it up, Col," she'd say to me as a child, "think of Jesus on the cross."

After a while, I read:

cmp

A Second Chance at Rainbows

Driving away from School 16, sad as this was my final session at the last of the five Troy elementary schools where I've been do a writing residency with all 4th graders in the district, my little Mini Cooper actually swayed from the gusty winds. Stopping for gas on Hoosick, dark clouds menacing, the wind lifted a garbage pail and hurled it into the street, nearly causing an accident.

"Crazy weather, huh?" a fellow gas-pumper called to me.

"Yes," I shouted back, the moment having a tornado-like Wizard of Oz feel.

Some had predicted today, 12-21-12, would be "doomsday" – interpreting ancient Mayan and other sources to mean it would be the end of the world. My brother, Jerry, is in Guatemala, joining many gathered to pray for world peace, love and enlightenment.

As I pulled into the Price Chopper parking lot, the DJ on the radio announced the striking of 26 bells, in memory of the 26 innocent people killed in Newtown. Turning off the ignition, I closed my eyes, and when the bells tolled, I prayed aloud: "peace, peace."

A minute later, I was picking out avocadoes in the produce aisle when someone ran in shouting to a friend: "Krista! Come see this. The most amazing rainbow ever!"

A rainbow right after the memorial. I considered going outside, but I had such a long list. Later, pushing the cart to my car, I searched the sky. No, I'd missed my chance. But then, at home in my kitchen, putting away the groceries, I looked out the window and saw the most gigantic, gorgeous rainbow…a magnificent arc over Frear Park, linking me to my mom up the hill. I picked up our cat, "Bro," to show her.

Sometimes we do get a second chance at rainbows.

* * *

"Well that's very good," my mother said, "very good."

I told Mom about how nice Christmas Eve day had been with my boys. I'd made a big breakfast, scrambled eggs, sausage, bacon, and cinnamon rolls and we lingered at the table talking, then moved to the living room. They opened their gifts from me; I opened my gifts from them. But for the first time I didn't get to see them give their presents to *each other* – always a special joy for me, because, to a fault, each stands up and moves to hug his brother. This Christmas they did that at "Dad's house."

On Christmas morning, Tony texted me to share how they were all opening presents together in front of the fireplace. Two hours later he texted to say they were all sitting around watching family video recordings he had transferred onto DVD's.

"I felt so sad and left out," I said, "missing all that reminiscing time with my boys… Halloweens, Easter egg hunts, Cape Cod trips…" I stopped as I was sobbing.

"I am so sorry, Col." Mom placed her warm hand over mine.

"It is what it is," I said. We sat in silence, looking out at the snow.

"I think all we can do is love and forgive," Mom said.

Later, she took the elevator downstairs with me as I left.

Outside, I turned back to see her turning the key in her mailbox.

I hope you have mail, Mom – a cheery letter, an invitation. I wish you had a partner, Mom, someone to share your life with. Who knows? Perhaps there is still time. Maybe if (secret name) comes to Mom's birthday party, he will invite her out on a date!

* * * * *

Week 5, January 4, 2013

Parks – Faith

Today would have been my father, Jerry Murtagh's, 78th birthday. He died in 1999 at the age of 64 from complications arising from his lifelong battle with alcoholism. Although we had been estranged for nearly two decades, thankfully near the end of his life, my Dad and I found a way to reconcile our relationship. One Christmas he came to visit my family at our home in Guilderland. It was the first and last time he would.

I'll never forget the sound of the doorbell ringing and then seeing him standing there…the smile on his face….the tears in his eyes, those beautiful blue eyes.

He brought his three young grandsons, Chris, Connor, and Dylan a "musical Christmas tree." It stood about two feet tall, with a plastic elf face, lips and eyes that moved when it sang: "*Oh what fun it is to be a baby Christmas tree. Oh! Hi there! It seems like only yesterday, I was just a pine cone…*"

My boys thought that was hysterical. They still do. Now some 15 years later, when someone hits that "Try Me!" button and the tree sings, they laugh and fondly recall that Christmas memory with their grandfather, and I am reminded that, for my father's faults, he had many fabulous qualities, too. For one thing, he was funny, *really funny*, and he took great delight in making other people laugh. I realize now what a rare gift that was. Oh how I would treasure just one more Christmas, just one more chat with him, especially now that I am a parent and very well aware of my own long list of shortcomings. He loved me the best way he knew how. That's all any of us can do.

⁂

Mom and I had lunch at my kitchen table by the window -- hummus on pita bread, vegetable soup, sliced apples, and Oreo cookies for dessert.

"I brought one of my poems," Mom said. "I had walked over from 2318 16th Street (the house she moved to with my siblings after separating from my father) to sit in Beman Park, the park of my childhood. Beman Park was *my park*." Then she read:

written in Beman Park, Sun. am, May 18, 1987

A Poem for My Park

I am here.
1987 – you can be a childhood year.
Because all the green of yesterday
is near ~
and yellow buttercups ~
and neglected dandelions ~
even their name holds no romance
for casual writers ~
I am here in Beman Park on a
splendid day.
Everything has changed – and
nothing (as we always say)
I don't recall a basketball court
then—in 1945—when I was
seven ~
and there was war.
Swings! Never a park for children
without swings.

We reminisced about some brave stupid
boy who went "over the bars."
Many like him before and after would
need to go all the way.
Buttercups ~ free and shining and ideal~
buttercups nodding
in beds of clover ~
and defining clover ~
You were shining then when I
was seven.
My old neighborhood ~
Why do I write of your altar ~
Beman Park
Because a constancy is here ~
One decade, one generation,
moving swiftly to another,
Movement stops here for a splendid
moment
And remembers.
Trees. Aging elms, maples ~
Would someone question how I call you?
Evergreens – some of you were here
when I was seven ~
And maybe some of you were seven, too
and we have aged together ~
Your leathered firmness does not try
to hide your aging marks ~
Nor your green leaves their "brand-new-ness."
Yesterday my park waited for me to
come in sandals and a sun suit
(we called them "sun suits") with a
peanut butter sandwich.
Forty years you waited for me to

remember my manners ~
Recall the gifts my mother taught me,
And my grandmother ~
To say, "thank you."

⁂

"That's just beautiful, Mom," I said. We talked some more and then I shared this:

cmp, 1-4-13

Faith

"Thank you, God, for this day," are the first words I spoke this morning, the first of many chats God and I will have today.

As we talk I feel *listened* to; I feel *loved*. That, to me, is faith.

Three Kodak photos slip out of my mind's childhood memory album:

My mother kneeling before the statue of Mary in May, rosary beads in hands.

My Dad leaving for 7:00 am Mass at St. Michael's before work every day during Lent.

My Nana at her kitchen table with a handful of prayer cards praying to her saints.

Watching these three main adults in my life during those growing up years, I *felt their faith*. It soaked into me and lodged in my soul.

Soon after college, though, I abandoned the Catholic religion of my youth. The whole women-can't-be priests, no woman's-right-to-choose, rich-Vatican-while-millions- are-starving stuff was more than my liberated self could stomach. When our boys were born, we did not get them baptized Catholic. It seemed hypocritical as we only went to church on Christmas and Easter. Now they call people like we were then "Chreasters."

Tony and I shopped for a church that "fit," finally settling on the First Unitarian Universalist Society of Albany (FUUSA). I liked the open hearts-open minds philosophy, respecting each person's spiritual journey, and there was a wonderful Religious Education program– encouraging lives of integrity and service – but when our oldest son, Chris, announced at 10 that he didn't believe in God, I felt horrible.

"Oh, no, Chris, there is a God," I rushed to assure him.

I told Tony we needed to head back to the Catholic Church, *pronto*. Christ the King Church was right up the street. The pastor, Fr. Pat Butler, was a good guy. I thought it would be so easy. It wasn't. My boys had to go through a nearly year-long preparation program. Several times we had to stand up on the altar, facing the congregation as people prayed for us. How embarrassing. I still laugh recalling Tony whispering in my ear on the altar: "I'm going to fucking kill you for this."

We could not have picked two religions more different than the Catholic Church and Unitarian-Universalism. "We're really going to screw up these boys," Tony said.

A lovely thing was that our sons got to choose their godparents. Chris picked his Aunt Noreen and Uncle Mike Mahoney. Connor chose Aunt Colleen and Uncle Kevin Murtagh. Dylan asked his grandmother, (Peg) "Tama", and his Uncle Jerry Murtagh.

Fast forward to this past Christmas, 2012. My three grown sons, Chris, 23, Connor, 20, and Dylan, 18, accompanied me to the 4 o'clock Christmas Eve Mass at Our Lady of Victory. They participated, sang the Christmas songs, and received Communion.

"You must be so proud of these young men," Fr. Randy Paterson (great guy) said.

"Oh my gosh, yes," I said, beaming. "I couldn't be more proud."

On Christmas morning at breakfast, Chris asked me if I ever go to FUUSA anymore. "I liked it there," he said. "I liked Christ the King, too. Father Pat was nice."

"Have you heard about this new church," Connor said. "I think it's in Latham. It's like a concert each week with big screens and a rock band…"

My sons were talking about religion. Maybe we didn't screw them up, after all.

"I've been going to three different churches," I said, "Our Lady of Victory, Metropolitan New Testament Baptist, Columbus's church, and Christ Church United Methodist downtown. There are two really inspiring women ministers there, Nina Nichols and Janet Douglass. I'm spreading my joy."

My sons laughed.

"I don't think I believe in God," Dylan said, "or heaven."

I nodded at my beautiful son, respecting that. "But I hope you have faith, Dyl."

"Oh yeah, Mom. For sure."

* * * * *

Week 6, January 8, 2013

Old-Fashioned Letters – Books

We had a booth by the window for lunch at Friendly's on Hoosick Street.

"I got the most beautiful letter," Mom said. It was from the daughter of a lady she'd connected with when they were both psychiatric in-patients at Four Winds Hospital in Saratoga. This came as no surprise as often when visiting my mother over the years during one of these stays, inevitably one, often more patients, will say how my mother was helping them more than any of the paid professionals.

"What I brought for our book was the letter I wrote back. Is that okay?"

"Sure," I said. "A from-your-heart letter is a universally encouraging thing."

Then my mother read:

Dear Ann,

First let me say thank you a million times for the Christmas card and most especially for your sincere words. I apologize for not responding sooner; I'm still battling my demons, trying to make positive choices and take positive steps into recovery.

I'll be 75 this month and it appears now (I'm a slow learner) I will have depression for the rest of my days. What I know is that I must not give up on myself. The dark side is real, but believing in myself is what I must remember to do ~ so Faith, Hope and Charity (love/caritas) are real, the stepping stones to help me walk the walk.

In November I began a writing project with my oldest daughter, Coleen – her suggestion, which I tried to avoid. Her plan: we get together once a week to share something we've written ~something positive –do it for a year – a mother/daughter project; so far we call it "Writing it Right" and then publish it. She's a published author and the idea is not financial, not about anything but sharing part of ourselves, so we'll see how it goes. Tonight as I write you this letter I have my weekly date with Coleen tomorrow at noon and have not yet written my piece – when we get together we read aloud what we've written.

Enough of that, Ann, but please know that your letter to me was inspirational and gives me a new hope. We (you and me and countless nameless sisters and brothers) indeed have something to share with each other – soulmate to soulmate – and you did that for me. Thank you for your words which I know come from your heart.

My soulmate/sister poet is Emily Dickinson; I'll quote for you one of my favorites:

Hope is the thing with feathers
that perches in the soul,
And sings the tune without the words,
And never stops at all.
And sweetest in the gale is heard;
And sore must be the storm

That could abash the little bird
That kept so many warm.
I've heard it in the chillest land,
And on the strangest sea;
Yet, never, in extremity,
It asked a crumb of me.

Dearest Ann,

I'll go now and write for my mother/daughter project. Go in peace and walk in God's love. Till we speak again,

Love, Peg ☺

"That's beautiful, Mom," I said.

"Thanks, Col," she said. "I need to get this to the post office." She took out her pocket calendar, flipping to the following week. "When do you want to meet again?"

"What about my piece?" I said.

"Oh, I'm sorry," she said and we laughed.

"No problem." I was so happy Mom was getting caught up in her own writing, her own *voice.* "I'll read quickly."

cmp, 1-8-13

Books

Ever since childhood, my most treasured material possessions have been *books.*

Two that immediately come to mind are *Simple Abundance*, by Sarah Ban Breathnach and *Bird by Bird*, by Anne Lamott – the margins of both are filled with my notations over the years, as I read their encouraging words, again and again.

My mother is totally to blame for my passionate love of reading. When I was little, we'd take the bus "uptown" to the Troy Public Library on Second Street. I'd stick my hand in the mouths of the lions in front of the County Court House, then push open the castle-heavy door of the Library to collect my treasures for the week.

The first book I remember owning, the first book I *saw myself in and loved* was a a beautifully illustrated edition of *Little Women*, by Louisa May Alcott, a tenth birthday gift from my godmother, Jane Spain Ducatt, a teacher and herself a talented writer.

I am also forever grateful to whoever (most likely a matchmaker librarian) handed me *Anne of Green Gables*, by Lucy Maud Montgomery. Decades later, this book would in great part inspire my first novel, *The Wedding Planner's Daughter*.

All through my early teen years I was a huge fan of Nancy Drew, saving up my money to purchase the newest release at Woolworth's on Third Street. Soon after, I moved on to Harlequin romances. At Catholic Central High School in Troy, Sr. Nancy Burkhardt introduced me to a bevy of great books ranging from Herman Hesse's inspirational *Siddhartha* to Ray Bradbury's magnificent *Fahrenheit 451*, about a high-tech future world where books are and burned. Bradbury once said: "Love is the answer to everything." It sounds like something my mother would say.

In the years earning my bachelor's in English from the College of Saint Rose and then my master's from Trinity, I had the pleasure of reading hundreds of great books and somewhere along the line developed a very good, or perhaps very bad, habit:

I cannot read a book without *writing* in it; to me they are twin endeavors. When I read, I always have a pen in my hand ready to write my reactions in the margins.

During all of the Mommy years when I diligently brought my sons to the Albany Public Library and then the Guilderland Public Library each week, I never checked out titles for myself because, as I emphasize when I share this habit of mine with the students I visit with in schools: "one never, *ever*, writes in a library book."

My character, Willa, is a huge book lover. In each novel, she talks about the books she is reading and posts her "Willa's Pix" list of favorites. Mom and I are compiling a recommended list of "encouraging books" to include at the end of our book.

Every book I *love* gets a spot in my home library. When I bought my Cape house, I had a carpenter build a wall of book shelves in the living room and brought half of my collection out there. Soon after though, back in Troy, I regretted that as often I'd be writing and want to refer to one of the books at the Cape house. This is a perfectly smart reason for purchasing an e-reader, which at the gentle but consistent urging of my son Connor, I finally broke down and did. My Kindle "Paperwhite" is being delivered today.

It's a small and silly consolation, but one nice thing about losing my Cape house is that I will soon have all my book babies back home here with me.

Virginia Woolf said that women who love books too much on earth may be disappointed when they reach heaven, imagining that God might tell St. Peter: "Look, these need no reward. We have nothing to give them here. They have loved reading."

* * * * *

Week 7, January 13, 2013

Favorite Quotes – Soul Sermons

Mom came to my house for tea at 3:00 pm. We were pressed for time as she was going to her "Prayer Group" (which I understand to be a gathering of liberal, mostly elderly, socially conscious Catholics, at least one priest and one former nun among the group, who meet monthly to share a service they take turns planning and hosting).

I was excited to tell her there's a play about Emily Dickinson entitled *The Belle of Amherst* at the East Greenbush Library on Jan 27 and that I had reserved two seats for us. This will be our first "artist's outing" since I took her to hear the Celtic Women perform at the Troy Music Hall in 2011. Mom had been way too depressed to enjoy it.

I had a long list of "book items" to share with Mom... feedback from author friends about titles...a list of possible publishers... places to hold our signing events...

Mom looked at her watch. "You're exhausting," she said. "I'm not you."

What? "I know," I said, hurt and annoyed. "I'm not asking you to be."

"I don't think I can do all of this," she said.

"These are just suggestions," I said, "ideas."

"Okay." Mom nodded. "Why don't you read first?" And so I did:

cmp, 1-13-13

Favorite Quotes

I collect inspirational quotes. My *Bartlett's Familiar Quotations* (17th edition)is filled with blue, pink and yellow sticky tabs marking lines I love. When I wrote my first novel, *The Wedding Planner's Daughter*, I decided to start each chapter with a quote from a favorite author. The first chapter, "The Wish," begins with this from Lewis Carroll's *Through the Looking Glass*:

"Why, sometimes I've believed in as many as
six impossible things before breakfast."

The final chapter, "Miracles," starts with this from Willa Cather:

"Where there is great love, there are always miracles."

As fans lovingly commented on the quotes, many saying they'd begun their own lists, "just like Willa," I kept it going throughout the series.

The walls of my writing room are covered with inspiring words. Here are a few:

"Be the change you want to see in the world."
Mahatma Gandhi

"See me beautiful, look for the best in me,
that's what I really am, and all I want to be..."
Kathy and Red Grammer

"If you get the inside right, the outside will fall into place."
Eckhart Tolle

"Where you stumble, there lies your treasure."
Joseph Campbell

"Life is either a daring adventure or it is nothing."
Helen Keller

Follow your heart's desire,
because that's the direction your spirit wants you to go."
(Pretty sure this is Oprah, I checked my new 18th Edition of *Bartlett's Familiar Quotations*, a thoughtful gift from my son, Connor, and was shocked to find not one single quote by Oprah Winfrey. *What? How can that be*? Shame on you, John Bartlett.)

I thank You God for this most amazing day:
for the leaping greenly spirits of trees and a blue true dream of sky;
and for everything which is natural which is infinite which is yes.
e.e. cummings

It takes as much energy to wish as it does to plan."
Eleanor Roosevelt

I fell in love with my imagination.
Alice Walker

To try and make the world in some way better
than you found it is to have a noble life.
Andrew Carnegie

The closer we get to giving our dream to the world,
the fiercer the struggle becomes to bring it forth.
Sarah Ban Breathnach

Do one thing every day that frightens you.
Eleanor Roosevelt

Embrace change ~ Befriend the person you are striving to become.
Joan Anderson

You're braver than you believe,
stronger than you seem, and smarter than you think...
A.A. Milne

How wonderful it is that nobody need wait a single moment
before starting to improve the world.
Anne Frank

The symbol for problem and the symbol for opportunity
is almost identical in Chinese.
Unknown

I have an attitude of gratitude. Nobody promised me this day.
Maya Angelou at her 82nd birthday party

If you ever have a new idea, and it's really new,
you have to expect that it won't be widely accepted immediately.
It's a long, hard process.

Rosalyn Yalow

Two roads diverged ... and I ... I took the one less travelled by
...and that has made all the difference.

Robert Frost

It is by spending oneself that one becomes rich.

Sarah Bernhardt

Knowledge puffs up, love builds up.

First Letter of Paul to the Corinthians

Nothing great was ever achieved without enthusiasm.

Ralph Waldo Emerson

Be not forgetful to entertain strangers,
for thereby some have entertained angels unawares.

Hebrews 13

...to know even one life has breathed easier because you have lived,
this is to have succeeded.

Ralph Waldo Emerson

Go confidently in the direction of your dreams.
Live the life you have imagined.

Henry David Thoreau

Tell me and I'll forget
Show me and I may not remember
Involve me, and I'll understand

Native American saying (author unknown)

Find the good and praise it.

Alex Haley

When I stand before God at the end of my life,
I would hope that I would not have a single bit of talent left,
and could say, 'I used everything you gave me.'

Erma Bombeck

* * *

After apologizing and lamenting that she was in a "really bad place" with her depression...she had a "code red" phrase for how *really bad* it was...my mother read:

psm, 1-13-13

Soul Sermons

It's Sunday morning and I'm here alone with my thoughts. Went to a wonderful party last night, a surprise 70th celebration for my sister Mimi, and the joy of all that – family, friends, food, singing all in Mim's honor is with me big time; what a blessing.

I'm trying to say something positive about my life. That, after all, is what I agreed to do with and for my daughter Coleen here in this writing effort. So excuse me if I ramble on. I'm still trying to figure out who I am, what I'm supposed to be doing. I don't think I've had an awakening, but it occurs to me I certainly have experienced a yearning. Yes, I feel it right now, a certain yearning, a yearning that doesn't go away.

And here's something certain about two things I know. One, I am a spiritual being searching for a way to live this human life. And two, I'm on my own path, but I'm not alone. Yes, I'm a dreamer, so what else is new? Eleanor Roosevelt is one of my great foremothers and great teachers. I didn't always know that about Eleanor but I certainly have known it for a long time. Eleanor said the future belongs to those who believe in the beauty of their dreams. That's an Eleanor wisdom for sure.

I feel the constriction of time which I always feel when I have to stop this typing soon and I could just go on and on. But I'm learning something about sensible scheduling and order and discipline from my daughter Coleen – yes we share gifts with each other. Here's a truth I know – I am learning a lot from my children, every one of them. It's part of why I don't give in to this temptation to just do nothing, or rest on your laurels as they say; I probably only have one or two laurels anyway, whatever that means.

This morning I was watching Oprah's Soul Sunday. I love what she's doing on her new OWN network, finding and working her spirituality and bringing countless spiritual teachers into our living rooms. Already this morning she's talked with Eckhart Tolle, made reference to Deepak Chopra, and interviewed the famous teacher, scholar, world traveler Jean Houston, herself a youthful 75 years of age. All in an hour's time; now that's motivation, Peg. They spoke also about Joseph Campbell who, in *The Power of Myth*, reminds us....now hear this: the privilege of a lifetime is being who you are.

That's worth saying again: The privilege of a lifetime is being who you are. I'm reminded again that there's so much to do, so much to be. The gift is with me today, at 75. Another piece of spiritual wisdom spoken this morning is the importance of being present to the depths and beauty of each and every person. I have many people of beauty in my life and a whole other world of beautiful people waiting.

Let me act in appreciation of the life I've been given.

That's my sermon to Peggy this Soul Sunday. Go in peace.

Week 8, Jan 24, 2013

Godmothers – "Firefly Ideas"

We met at 3:00 pm for tea at Mom's. She served our favorite orange, passion fruit and jasmine green tea along with Susanna's Natural Strawberry Gourmet Shortbread Cookies purchased at Uncle Sam's, a health food store, on 4th Street downtown.

The music was the "play list" of Mom's favorite songs which my sister, Nor, had so thoughtfully compiled for her 75th birthday party last Saturday at The Park Pub. Mom showed me some of the cards and gifts she'd received. My siblings and I had overruled Mom's explicit plea for "no gifts, please," suggesting in the invitation that a gift of "time with YOU" would be a nice gesture, our motive being to get Mom out more.

Gifts included I.O.Us for dinners out and movie dates. Her dear friend Terry Paige offered "3 walks together," including a "walk around the northern part of the Frear Park golf course" and a "surprise walk." My mother has the most wonderful friends – brilliant, kind, and fun to be around.

"The Rose" by Bette Midler came on and a wave of sad nostalgia hit me. This was the song Tony and I danced our "first dance" to at our wedding reception in 1980 with 360 relatives and friends in attendance. In 2005 my beautiful sister-in-law Colleen McNulty Murtagh sang "The Rose" acappella at our 25th Anniversary Renewal of Vows at the Popponesset Inn on Cape Cod. Three years later, we would be separated.

This week, Mom's contribution for our "good" book is an ode to her godmother, Josephine Spain, who raised 7 children, Joseph, Edward, Johnnie, Danny, Mary, Michael, and Anthony in a house on Burdette Avenue in Troy, near Samaritan Hospital.

psm, 1-18-13

Peg's Note: Twenty years ago – January 18, 1993 – I had a second heart attack and was in the CCU at Samaritan Hospital. My Aunt Jo was also a patient there; something I had not been told so as not to "upset" me. I found out when I had an unannounced visit from a woman who had just brought Communion to my aunt and thought she'd stop by and see me. My Aunt Jo and I were always very close. I used to visit her and we'd talk; she was my godmother, like a mother to me all those years when my own mother and I were separated. When the visitor left my room I cautiously got out of bed and made my way down the hall to my aunt's room. I found her sleeping and looking very weak and frail. I thought we would lose her soon. I did not disturb her but quietly walked back to my room. With feelings of love and concern, I penned these words.

Sorry I Missed You Aunt Jo

Irish eyes that sparkle
Irish laughter singing to you
You could love the Irish
If you knew my Aunt Jo.
Neat
Down home in the finest sense,
She welcomed you,
More a welcomer than a hostess
(If you get my drift)
She made you feel at home.

I knew this way back when
I was a young girl
just old enough to take Dan to the park,
our park
Beman Park
in the stroller.

And got to stay for supper
which turned out to be dinner
(if you get my drift)

roast beef, dark gravy
mashed potatoes,
French green beans,
and cake,
cake so chocolate you knew
you couldn't be all bad
so rich were the gifts of her kitchen.

What's the point of a poem
I don't know
It's just my thing
Some feeble attempt
A mile off target (if you get my drift)
To say something pure and simple
about a woman pure and simple.

Always there.
The thing is she was always there
Even when she wasn't home
Which wasn't often,
And I would leave a note a her door,
"Sorry I missed you"
And she would call and say,
"Sorry I missed you."

An Irish mother who never kept a ledger
of accounts receivable;
Never called in a debt,
and there were many
mine alone were countless.

You could love an Irish mother
If you knew my Aunt Jo.

Whatever pain or joy sent me
running to her door
to her kitchen
to the sanctuary of grace and blessing
and sacramental love
undefiled by price tag
poured over like tea or coffee
and healing my wounds
and sealing my joy

And now we're here
In this same place
You and I the same
Sick of heart
Breaking down
And I want to sit at your kitchen table
And hear your lilting laughter

And I fear I won't again
Except in my heart's secret place
And if that is to be
That is to be (if you get my drift)

Sorry I missed you Aunt Jo
And glad I knew you
You made me better than I am.

From a loving godchild
Peg Spain Murtagh

⁂

Mom talked about her Aunt Jo some more, and when it was my turn, I read this:

cmp, 1-24-13

"Firefly Ideas"

Soon after my first book was published, I coined the phrase "firefly ideas" to describe those moments when an intriguing new thought *sparks* inside, bright as a firefly on a summer night.

Firefly ideas are a source of great joy for me, a reason to move through the day with anticipation. I never know when one will spark and that is so *exciting*.

At my author visits to schools, I wave this tiny blinking gummy ring in the air and ask the students, "Have you ever seen a bit of light zip past you on a summer night?"

Many hands shoot up excitedly.

"What are they?" I ask.

"Lightning Bugs! Fireflies!"

"Right," I say. "And maybe you run inside for an empty jar, poke some holes in the lid, and run back out to catch one." I pick up the clear plastic jar with a yellow lid that I bought at a Dollar Store before my first author visit in 2004 and now take with me everywhere I talk about writing, pop the "firefly" inside, close the lid and hold it up high. "Look," I say. "Isn't that spark of light amazing?"

The students nod, staring. They are all with me in the moment.

"It....is....just...that...way...with... *ideas*," I say.

"Fireflies *surprise* us. So do firefly ideas."

I wait while they think about that. "Now, if I am a writer and I catch a firefly *idea*, what should I do right away, fast as I can, so I won't lose it?"

"Write it down," some will call out.

"Louder," I say.

"Write it down," they'll shout.

"Three times to remember," I say.

"WRITE IT DOWN, WRITE IT DOWN, WRITE IT DOWN."

The sound is exhilarating. As it should be. Ideas are exciting. Writing is exciting. If I only ever teach one true thing about writing it is this: "Catch ideas like fireflies on a summer night and write what *only you* can write."

* * * * *

Week 9, January 31, 2013

Birthday Parties – Positive Energy People (PEPs)

We drove downtown to the Ilium Café on Broadway for lunch. At a quiet table for two by a window and fireplace, we ordered crabmeat sliders and the ahi tuna and avocado salad. Mom noted that our waiter, Cordell, was handsome. I concurred. Mom told me how happy she was that I had found love in my life with Columbus.

"It's not too late for you, Mom," I said. "You're so pretty and smart." A perfect segue, I handed her a clipping from the *New York Times* "Modern Love" page about a couple who fell in love and announced their engagement at their "joint 150th birthday party" the year she turned 70 and he, 80, and then married a year later.

"It can happen, Mom," I said. "You just need to put yourself out there."

My mother shook her head, laughing. "That's easy for you to say."

I wondered why (secret name) didn't show up for her birthday. His loss.

"Well, I brought two things," Mom said. "The piece I wrote the morning of my 75th birthday, and then what I wrote that night." Cordell escorted Mom to check out the dessert display case where she chose a piece of blueberry pie and upon returning read:

psm, 1-20-13

Toward Healing

I'm grateful I have in my possession some past years' journals; I need them right now when the winter doldrums are trying to bring me down. They remind me that my journey toward healing continues. This entry I wrote 17 years ago; it sounds so like me because it *is* me. Yes, I'm still struggling – but today at 75, with the value of hindsight, my journey is toward healing. Thank you, Col, for encouraging me to *write me right.*

Monday, January 29, 1996, 7:16 am

I need to look at the meditations of Hildegard this morning: too much confusion, disappointment, even the ugly heads of guilt and shame trying to get at me. Scanning the table of contents I choose Meditation 7, Wellness: The Call to Choose Life; opening prayer: *I pray to you, God, the strength of my life, for gentle healing and fullness of life.* I tend not to give myself credit for what good I am able to do, and I tend to deride myself too harshly for what I do that is not good and for what good I fail to do. Hildegard says that God has blessed us with *viriditas,* "the greening power of life," and desires that we *nurture ourselves to wellness.* The simplicity of wisdom. God within me. The co-mingling of the human and the divine. A call to the good life is first a call to prayer. How else to proceed but to bow in wonder, awe, honor and respect before the Divine Love, the Word of God. I pray to you, God, the strength of my life, for gentle healing and fullness of life. So many things call to me, in my mind; and my body suffers from my neglectfulness. So first I bow acknowledging God's infinite love and compassion. The gift of fullness of life, offered in God's desire that I nurture myself to wellness. See, hear and feel, Peggy.

I forgot to go to Confirmation rehearsal at 7 last night (editorial note, Peg was working for Christ Sun of Justice, the Catholic community at RPI at the time). I can speculate why. "Out of sync" comes to mind. How easy to fall into a neglectful mode. How easy to deprive Peggy of proper care and nourishment. It's so easy I scare myself, realizing how easy it can be to lose myself. Here is a new day, a new week. A challenge, a gift, an offering to accept, and cherish. I eat a healthy carrot/raisin muffin from Coleen who says "I don't want you to eat 'Spam'." The sun is shining, snow is predicted. Mary's (co-worker) daughter Karen has a houseful of gifts for her baby, to be born in March. Spring will come. Dr. Wasserman will treat my toenails at 9 am. Lyn (a friend) is in Albany Med psych ward, healing slowly. I had fun with Christopher (grandson) who was taking his bath and then showing me his map and globe – all the countries he can locate --- talking about my project – Africa – and his – Australia. Yesterday a.m. did my Prime Time Aerobics workout – it was fun and good for me.

Life proceeds. I can care deeply for Peggy today. The young girl in the Christmas photograph has lived now to her 58th year, and is continuing on her journey. She wants to be a college graduate. She can do nothing alone. She is not alone. But I am responsible – to respond. To not neglect. To care. To think. To act in love with the gift of my mind, the heart, the soul. *Veriditas*, the greening power of life, speaks of the promise of spring even as winter continues. Send apologies to Tom (her boss at the time) and offer assistance. Contact St. Rose re tuition bill payment – give them an opportunity to be helpful as you endeavor to help Peggy move along on her labor of love journey. Life is a gift from an All-Loving God. Amen.

psm, 1-20-13

My Birthday Party on 1/20/13

Note: I can't even begin to express the fullness of emotion filling my heart when I recall that special day when I turned 75 and my children gifted me with a party. At the end of that day, I wrote down what I recalled of the event; nothing eloquent, just a remembering. Coleen thought I should write something about my birthday so I read what I had written in my journal and she said it should go in our book. I hope I can write something sometime worthy of that once in a lifetime happening; but for now here's what I wrote (with nothing edited) in my journal.

Sunday, January 20, 2013, 10:40 pm

My children gifted me with a 75th birthday party and as I focus on the smiling and joy filled faces of children, spouses, grandchildren, siblings and friends, I'm grateful in a full and happy way. Coleen was the (and I'll say ringleader for lack of a more complimentary word). Noreen brought music, a music machine with a mike, balloons, table decorations, candies. By music I mean she asked me to let her know some of my favorite old songs and she turned them into (burned?) recordings and saw to it that music played the whole time we were there at the Frear Park Pub back room. Special friends Bill and Alice McL, Martha Walsh, Terry Page, and Mary Jane Smith. All so pleasant and gracious to my family. All kinds of great food, salad, pizza, sausage and peppers, many varieties of wings, veggie tray, fruit and cheese and crackers, soda, beer & wine; I'll just ramble on, tables covered with birthday paper cloths. Danny and Liane, Mike, Nor & Jack, Col, Columbus, Chris, Connor & Dylan, Jerry right off the bus from NY (Chris picked him up), my brother Charlie (Jim was just home from the hospital – an infection something serious in his blood), my sisters Janie, Virginia, Mim – did I name everyone, Kevin, Colleen, Liam, Lauren, Brendan – Colleen Murtagh McNulty made 2 from scratch cakes – an ice cream cake and dark chocolate with mocha frosting – candles lit on both cakes – she had called me earlier in the week wanting to know what kind of cake I liked best – can you imagine? After we ate Coleen asked us to sit in a (large, oblong) circle and with the mike passed around – everyone said something positive and very complimentary about me. We sang, I sang, others – Nor, Col, Janie, Ging, Mim joined in. Jack thanked me for Canasta, as did Chris, Dyl, and others I'm sure I'm missing. The party was at 3 o'clock – no snow, roads clear, cold and windy and people all seemed to have a good time. Columbus was right there, helping Col, being a nice, gentle man and singing to me when it was his turn on the go around the room.

Later, back in my apt., Jer and I relaxed. I ate more of Coll's delicious cake, caught some of Oprah's interview with Lance Armstrong. Then

Jerry gave me a gift of ascended masters reading cards and we did a reading and Jer helped me light a candle. He gave me a special Eagle (?) feather, something you light and enjoy the aroma (I can't remember the name); some of my cards were Michael the Archangel, Jesus on love, Joy (Buddha). I want to open cards, maybe tomorrow and write thank you notes.

Everything was special, beautiful, all for me – I am touched.

⁂

We talked about both of Mom's pieces and then I read this:

cmp, 1-31-13

"Positive Energy People" (PEP's)"

There are certain people in the world who seem abundantly gifted with *light*. They exude such enthusiasm, such positive energy that when you're in their presence, you feel sparked, charged, enlightened, too. These Positive Energy People, "PEP's," are so full of light they magnetically draw forth the light in you. They see what is good and *possible*. They reflect your best self back to you like a marvelous motivating mirror.

My friend *Corey Jamison* jumps to mind. President of a successful consulting company, mother/stepmother of 7 children ranging in age from toddler to high school aged, flamboyantly fashionable, Zumba dancing, annual Avon marathon fundraiser (in honor of her mother, Kaleel, who died of breast cancer), studying for her PHD, Corey lights a room like the 4th of July. She does this by being the biggest Corey she can be.

Denise McCoy owned The Bookmark in Loudonville. In the years I was trying to get published, Denise was an indefatigable cheerleader. When I shared the news, over lunch at Milano's, that I had *finally* gotten a contract, Denise's eyes lit with joy: "I'm going to throw a big launch party for you!" Denise died before that could happen. At the funeral home, I waited two hours in a long line of mourners to pay my respects, a visible testament to just how many people Denise had touched with her great spark.

Micki Nevett was the beloved librarian at Westmere Elementary School. She took great delight in encouraging new writers and had very high standards for excellence. When Micki said she "loved" my book, *Sunny Holiday*, I cried I was so proud. After Micki died of a heart attack while serving on the Newbery Committee (charged with naming the best children's book of the year), devastated by her loss, we on the Children's Literature Connection board created a tribute in her honor. "The Sparkler Award" is given annually to a person whose joy for reading is an inspiration to all.

My friend *Judy Barnes* bursts next to mind. Talented author and head of a thriving communications consulting business-- when Judy's silvery haired, sparkly dressed self enters a room, preceded by her quintessential effervescent hallmark laugh – you need to put on sunglasses, Judy's light is just so bright.

I could go on and on, but will stop here at the risk of leaving too many friends out. I am so very lucky have so many PEP's in my life.

Yesterday, I took Mom to see "The Belle of Amherst," majestically performed by Sara Melita. While watching the performance, it struck me that although Emily Dickinson is often thought of as a recluse, she sparkled with joy as she talked about her family, the buds on the trees, the bird on the branch by her window. I sensed that anyone lucky enough to have been her friend would have felt absolutely *showered with light*.

Seeing my mother nodding appreciatively in the front row (someone left at intermission and I zipped up to claim this seat for her), I thought despite how crippled she's been with depression, how beaten down with that daily darkness, she still strives to maintain a sunny disposition, to note the good in others....to be a light, to draw out light.

Emily Dickinson would have *loved* my mother.

Week 10, February 6, 2013

Hometowns – Comfort Foods

We met for lunch at Manory's on 4th and Broadway, the "oldest restaurant in Troy," this year celebrating its 100th anniversary. The charm of the place is that it never seems to change. It's just as I remember it coming here for tuna fish sandwiches with my Nana as a child. Popular with the local poor and politicos alike, it's had such famous visitors as Hillary Clinton, Michelle Pfeiffer, and The Red Hot Chili Peppers. It's is one of my favorite Troy places. My sons like it, too.

Mom was waiting in a well-worn cracked green leather booth by the window. She ordered a crab-meat salad sandwich -- me, the tuna fish.

"I wrote about Troy," Mom said and read this:

psm, 2-6-13

Speaking of Troy

I'm drawn to speak of my city – its place in my heart – not because I'm any kind of an expert on Troy's history. Troy's history is grand and glorious and well worth coming to know. As far back as I can remember my father told us our city's name came from Greece, and like the ancient city, Troy was built on I think it was seven (or six) hills; Mount Ida and Mount Olympus come first to mind. I was born in the Samaritan Hospital on January 20, 1938 (yes that makes me 75) and my hospital still stands in the same location a stone's throw from Beman Park. It's been added to and modernized over the decades, but those grand pillars of the original structure -- Ionic or Corinthian -- still remain erect and flawless. And even today, every time I drive up People's Ave from 15th to Burdett my eyes are pleasured again as I see them, these same pillars that my mother admired and my father. You know, you can be a child again if you've lived to 75 and can still walk around your old neighborhood, old home town. Imagine, I can sit in my park and look at my hospital and experience the enriching texture of my roots.

The big structures I remember are School 17 at the corner of 16th and Hutton and St. Paul's Church at 12th and Hutton both childhood cathedrals where I learned to read and write and learn about God. And there were other buildings, smaller than my school and church but no less real to me. One was the Arrow Cash Market on 15th Street where I walked across the vacant lot from my house at 1511 Hutton St. carrying those precious wartime ration coupons, feeling very grown up at maybe 6 or 7 on an errand to pick up a few groceries for my mother. And the other building on the corner of 15th and Hutton, just a few doors down from our house, McGrane's corner store, a favorite hangout of the older boys (the names Turk Mulqueen and Whiskey Dundon come to mind), guys so handsome and grown up and puffing cigarettes, posing in a squat-like position and paying no attention whatsoever to me. I have a vague memory of carrying a small piece of white paper, some numbers scratched on it; I think it was called playing the numbers. This delivery to McGrane's was grown up business and never discussed with me.

So Beman Park was my neighborhood and Beman Park was my park, but my Troy journey would move me to another neighborhood at the bottom of Eagle St. when my father returned from World War II. There I would go to St. Peter's church and school (I remember the nuns emphasized it was St. Peter's *Academy*, not school, and I have this kaleidoscope in my mind of other scenes, one about the nuns telling us to always say Hello, never say "Hi" " because saying Hi was too mindful of Hitler. Or how the nuns emphasized and, don't you forget it, that our music teacher was much more than a teacher -- she was a *Doctor*, a Professor of Music. And how Miss Anna Mae Marvelli came from her dance studio downtown to our Lyceum (another St. Peter's word) to teach us how to dance, Sister Hilda insisting that all her seventh graders learn to waltz, polka and fox trot.

Imagine for a minute a big street map of Troy, and a box of colored pinpoints where I can mark every place I have walked or bussed to within my city's limits (there were two bus companies, the familiar yellow and red United Traction Company and the other brown fleet for going north to Lansingburgh.) And there were movie houses all over the place. My first movie memory is on Hoosick St. when Hoosick St. was just busy Hoosick St. before it was turned into a major six-lane thoroughfare heading Route 7 to Bennington, Vermont. In the late 1940s and early 1950s we Spain kids, 5 of us anyway (Jim was a baby, born in 1948, and he had to stay home with Mom) walked to the corner of Fifth Ave. and Hoosick, to the Palace Theatre where for a 12 cent admission each we got all this: two full length features, the weekly serial (The Lone Ranger, Roy Rogers/Dale Evans, maybe Gene Autry); then the week's news in review (home TV was still in its infancy), that's not all, several cartoons (Elmer Fudd, Mickey Mouse) and finally the previews of things to come, "see you next week." To say the least, it was a full afternoon's entertainment for the Spain kids, and a very big deal to be sure.

There were any number of other theatres, mostly downtown. We went in small groups, 3 or 4 couples, all grown up now in 7th and 8th grade, and we had our choice of either the medium priced Griswold or American, or the higher priced Troy Theatre or famed former vaudeville house Proctors (those last two cost 25 cents). Uptown maybe at 112th St. there was The Bijou and I think there was a Strand south of downtown. It was the fifties and these were the glory days of cities and movies.

And the people. I don't have enough pinpoints for all the people. Before downtown was prematurely laid to rest with the ill-fated Atrium (mall) it was a Friday or Saturday night downtown of standing room only. Teens had their favorite hangouts: Paul's, The Puritan, Manory's, more than just a few pizza parlors including The Red Front or The Volcano. And on Friday you could shop till 9:00 pm at one of the you-name- it retail stores, like maybe, Denby's, Peerless, Muhlfelder's, the Up-To-Date, Weinberg's and don't forget Stanley's where you had three floors of moderate prices, and where right into the 1970s I was still shopping for my son Michael's boy scout uniform and lots of other bargains for my six children.

And churches, more pinpoints, oh how I remember churches. One trek when I was probably 11 or 12 and we -- good pre-Vatican II Catholic kids -- honored a Holy Thursday tradition and visited Troy churches (accent on the plural). After St. Peter's, we walked to St. Anthony's, St. Lawrence, St. Mary's, St. Joseph's, St. Jean's, Holy Trinity and almost but not quite to St. Michael's, then on Stow Ave. (I'd be in that parish when I married and moved to 16 High St.) All in all on that Holy Thursday we walked about 20 blocks, thought nothing of it except to feel as I've already said, like very holy, very good Catholic kids.

In my reverie I pinpoint churches, movie theatres, retail stores, bus lines and that's only an inch of my Troy journey. I remember being a high school freshman or sophomore, being honored with other winners of the Elks city- wide contest for highschoolers, to create your version of A Portrait of the American Flag. Mine was an essay (I wish I had it today). I stood on the mayor's podium on that Flag Day in Barker Park, at the corner of Third and State Sts., accepting the second place bronze plaque. (First prize as I recall was a most impressive painting by a student at Troy High.)

Decades later in the 80s when I was Director of Joseph's House (homeless shelter), we received a monetary gift of several thousand dollars, the final balance at the closing of St. Lawrence's, one of the many churches I had visited on a long ago Holy Thursday, one of many fated to be closed in the future, including my own St. Paul's and my own St. Peter's. At the time I visited houses of worship of various other denominations -- Episcopal, Baptist, Lutheran, Methodist, Presbyterian and at least two synagogues – always telling the story of Joseph's House, then located at 1 St. Paul's Place, on the corner of Fourth and State Sts.

Speaking of Troy, I have always been and intend to always be a Troy girl. For a few brief years at the beginning of this new century I moved to Green Island and lived on Hudson Avenue where my back yard faced the Hudson River and across the river my hometown. I have pleasant memories of that time, the McNulty family treated me like family, but in time I became increasingly homesick and in 2006 moved into Troy Housing at 12 Conway Court and here I am. My heartspeak tells me I'm home to stay.

* * *

"Mom, this is terrific!" I said. "You should send it to Lisa Lewis (editor at the *Troy Record)* and the Mayor (Lou Rosamilia)." Then I read:

cmp, 2-6-13

"Comfort Foods"

Perhaps because Sunday was the Super Bowl and in America that means "pizza and wings," I've been thinking about how food not only fuels us, but makes us feel loved.

When I was a child home sick from school, Mom made "Lady Fingers" – buttered white toast, sprinkled with cinnamon sugar, cut into strips and served with tea.

There was always turkey on Thanksgiving, roast beef on Christmas, corned beef on St. Patrick's Day, ham on Easter. On New Year's Eve Mom served fancy appetizers, my favorite was a sautéed sausage, mushrooms, and herb mixture served on triangles of toast.

With 6 children and an evening job outside the house, too, Mom's weekday meal repertoire was standard "big family" fare: chili with corn bread, spaghetti and meatballs, baked meatloaf topped with ketchup, served with mashed potatoes, peas and carrots.

My Nana who lived downstairs from us, delighted in making breakfast for me any morning I rapped on her kitchen window. I rapped a lot. We were always the first ones up. Bacon and eggs, pancakes and sausage, Cream of Wheat, oatmeal with raisins, Danish pastries from Nelligan's bakery, and tea, pots and pots of Lipton tea.

Occasionally Nana would walk up the "inside staircase" to our floor and knock on our living room door with a plate of delicious, nut-filled square "Refrigerator Cookies," as she called them, or a pan of Jello filled with fruit cocktail, peaches, or sliced bananas.

When my three boys were little, I loved making cinnamon sugar topped banana bread for them and oatmeal raisin cookies and Jello jigglers cut in various shapes depending on the season, red hearts in February, green shamrocks in March. When we moved to Guilderland, our wonderful neighbor, Lois Pasternak, brought over a plate of buttery blond cookies with raspberry preserve centers. We fell in love. Chris dubbed them "Lois's cookies." After Lois gave me the recipe, I tried substituting low-calorie margarine for butter and they never tasted quite as good as the real "Lois's cookies."

All those years the boys were growing up, I cooked dinner for our family each week night, generally healthy recipes, lots of fresh vegetables and grilled chicken dishes, with the occasional meatloaf with mashed potatoes or chili with cornbread. Christmas Eve was an "hors d'oeuvre" party on blankets spread in front of the fireplace with every kind of junk-food item the boys requested – chicken fingers, pizza bagels, mini hotdogs, chips and dips, and such. For twenty three years, Tony and I hosted an annual family Christmas party where everyone brought a dish to share and there were prizes for the "favorites." And while many relatives outdid themselves with gourmet offerings, it was always a given that "Aunt Mary's (Fox) Meatballs," Swedish meatballs, would win.

On Christmas mornings as Tony helped the boys assemble their toys, I would make a big breakfast -- scrambled eggs, sausage and bacon, Pillsbury Cinnamon Rolls smothered in frosting, and mugs of hot cocoa with marshmallows.

My friend Kathy Johnson showed up one Christmas-time with a container of the most delicious fudge ever. "Kathy's Fudge" became a tradition we looked forward to. For years I thought it must be some laborious process to make something so delicious. When I finally asked Kathy for the recipe, she laughed and said, "One word.... Fluff."

Sure enough, there was the fudge recipe right on the Fluff jar in the baking aisle.

Smile. I made a batch the following year, but it didn't taste as good as "Kathy's Fudge."

My mother is known for her chopped chicken liver pate which she spreads on Ritz crackers and squeezes with lemon juice as a Thanksgiving Day appetizer and for a delightfully rich (think sour cream) dessert called "Peg's Texas Brownie."

Columbus loves sweet potato pie and German chocolate cake. My sister, Nor, an *amazing* cook, she should have her own show, made a sweet potato pie from scratch this Thanksgiving and everyone raved about it. I've wanted to surprise Columbus with a German chocolate cake, but holey-moley, who has the time?

My author friend Rose Kent emailed me the solution to the German chocolate cake problem. Lo and behold Betty Crocker has a German chocolate cake mix AND the frosting to match. Hooray! I made it for Super Bowl Sunday dessert and it was great. Thank you Rose and Betty.

These days I do much less cooking -- healthy frozen dinners, take out, salads and grilled salmon or chicken. There is turkey on Thanksgiving, usually at my sister's house; a brunch with ham on Easter; corned beef at one of Troy's great Irish pubs on St. Patty's Day. Christmas Eve is still an "hors d'oeuvre party" with all the boys' favorites and new additions, like the hot taco dip that was a hit this year. That recipe is now tucked into the "Christmas" section of the orange binder in my kitchen labeled "Col's Cookbook." The Desserts section features the recipes for "Nana's Refrigerator Cookies" and "Kathy's Fudge" and "Peg's Texas Brownie" and "Lois's Cookies," and "Col's Caribbean Banana Bread." I added "Caribbean" to make it sound more exotic.

Yesterday, after Chris and I saw the movie, *Lincoln*, now that football season is officially over, I got the idea to invite him over for a "family dinner" on Sunday.

"Sure Mom, sounds good."

"What would you like me to make?" I hesitated, worried that there wouldn't be something he'd remember me making, no "comfort food" associated with me.

"Anything, Mom. Whatever you want."

"How about meatloaf?" I said.

"Great. I love your meatloaf."

My meatloaf. I have a meatloaf. I nearly cried with joy.

"With mashed potatoes," Chris said.

When I told Dylan we're going to have a family dinner Sunday at 5:30 and that I was making meatloaf he said, "I like your meatloaf." *Yay. He remembers, too!*

"What would you like for dessert?" I asked.

"Make that cake," Dylan said.

"What cake?"

"The one you made for the Super Bowl. It's my favorite."

I love ya, Betty.

⁂ ⁂ ⁂ ⁂ ⁂

Week 11, February 14, 2013

Bless My Heart - Kismet

We met for lunch at the The Broadway Café after reading an article in the *Troy Record* quoting owner Christine Carpinello saying she took "pride in being a part of a growing community of women owned businesses in downtown," and how that was a "lesson and legacy" she hoped to pass on to her own daughter. Mom and I wanted to honor that intention by supporting her new restaurant.

"It's Valentine's Day," Mom said, "so I wrote about the heart."

psm, 2-14-13

Bless My Heart

When all is said and done, what is there that makes any sense at all? This is the month of hearts and valentines. I struggle to get to the bottom line of life's valentine to me. If I were to write a valentine to myself, it would say something about the true meaning of love. Who do I love? Who loves me? I guess I know that in my long life every heart break and every heart mend has taught me this bottom line lesson – love has saved you. If I'm still alive I've been given another chance to reopen my heart and heal; heal myself, and give something of myself to someone in need of healing.

There certainly have been men in my life who have offered me unconditional love. In the big Spain family I had many aunts, uncles and cousins, but let me tell you about just one, my Uncle Walt, one of my father's older brothers. It's 1953, I'm 15 and on this day I've experienced an emotional family trauma and an ambulance has been called to bring me to the Albany Hospital psych ward.

I'm lying face down on the living room floor, very still, frightened, not knowing what's going to happen to me. I'm aware that others are around but I sense only the presence of one -- my Uncle Walt -- who has knelt down beside me. In my mental fear and anguish, I hear myself saying, "Do you love me, Uncle Walt?" And right away he offered his unconditional gift of love to me as I heard him say, "You bet I do, honey."

Love means sharing a piece of your heart, a valentine offered, a mending. The miracle of my life has been this coming to know that it is love that heals. I've known my heart breaking down, heart attack, open heart surgery. I've been opened up and put back together more than once. There have been doctors, in hospitals, who have blessed my heart and so the bottom line of my life has everything to do with who has loved me enough to care, to help me heal. Uncle Walt's loving was up close, it was real, he blessed my heart and I was able to accept the gift into my heart.

So we know, I know, that the love gift is surely not the perfect Hallmark card, the imported Swiss chocolate, the beautiful flowers by wire although such offerings can be love tokens. Men have loved me, women have loved me and children have loved me and it's this very human experience, this breathing in, this knowing of this unconditional love that keeps my heart mending and allows me to return this same love. Love is the bottom line, it is love that heals the broken heart and so I bless my heart, the mended vessel of my love as I bless yours. Happy Valentine's Day. Bless your heart.

"That's so beautiful, Mom," I said. "What a gift you are giving here."

We chatted for a while and then I read:

cmp, 2-14-13

Kismet

"It's *kismet*," editor Judy O'Malley said to me.

She had critiqued a manuscript of mine at a Society of Children's Book Writer's and Illustrators retreat in the Poconos when I was first breaking in to the field. Judy liked the story. We connected as people. *I would love to work with her*. It was the first time I heard the word, "kismet," which means *fate* or *destiny*, or some might say, *luck*.

"This is beautiful," Judy said, of my story about a young boy and his Mom and a Cape Cod sunrise, inspired by my son, Dylan, on the morning of his seventh birthday.

"I can see Peter Catalanotto (noted illustrator) doing the paintings," Judy said.

When I got home, I wrote KISMET on a sticky label and posted it at the top of my computer screen. I revised the manuscript according to Judy's suggestions, but then put it aside as I began working on other books.

The following spring, after reading that Peter Catalanotto would be a presenter, I went back to that same weekend retreat and sought a chance to speak with him. Peter agreed to read the manuscript and a few weeks later emailed to say he was interested. I contacted Judy O'Malley post haste and that's how *Catching the Sun* came to be.

Since today is Valentine's Day I will share another "kismet" story:

Three years ago, I was out with my dear friends Ellen Donovan and Kathy Johnson celebrating Ellen's birthday. We went to Creo's restaurant in Albany for dinner then to "Rafferty's" in Latham for dancing. I had never been there before.

When we arrived, Rafferty's was crowded, music booming. Immediately I spotted this tall handsome man standing by the DJ booth, smartly dressed in a suit and tie, eyes closed, head and shoulders moving to the beat.

"Bye," I said to my girlfriends, and walked straight across the room to him.

I stood staring up at his face, heart pounding.

After a few moments he said, "Are you looking at me?"

"Yes," I nodded, smiling.

"Well it's my lucky day," he said, and we danced.

We danced the whole night long.

We're still dancing, Columbus and me.

It will be three years on March 27.

Kismet.

Week 12, February 20, 2013

From Darkness to Light – Right Work

We met for lunch at Spill'n the Beans on 3rd Street, a popular restaurant a few doors down from our wonderful Troy independent bookstore, Market Block Books.

Mom read first:

psm, 2-20-13

From Darkness to Light

I feel the pressure and stress of not being ready (writing something positive) for my weekly get-together with Col tomorrow.

If procrastination is one of my major- not- minor shortcomings, well that's putting it mildly. I'll tell you one thing though, this gift of faith, this knowing belief in a God who loves me unconditionally, carries me through the darkness even when I'm afraid and can't see where I'm going. So let me say something positive and watch the negative, the darkness, turn my lights on.

My life has come in stages of death and rebirth, and I do believe I could never have come into blessed soul healing had I not felt, really felt the dark moments. To reiterate those agonies in my garden (trust me they hurt) is not my intent here. The point is this: I know that life is a celebration and I can't help breathing a prayer of gratitude that I'm still here to say thank you, indeed to be (emphasis on *be*), every day, that prayer of gratitude. So, if Peggy asks Peggy, "who are you?" or "what are you?", my one true answer is: I am a prayer of gratitude.

On Sunday I went to The Dutch Reformed Church on New Scotland Avenue and heard and saw and experienced, up close and personal, a beautiful man, Father Roy Bourgeois, MM. Roy is my most recent example of how you can turn darkness into light. The Roman Catholic Church, my church, Roy's church, has stripped him of his priesthood; forbidden him to speak out write out act out (as if they could do that) because of his open support of a woman's right to be ordained. Rome says Roy can no longer be Roy, no longer a priest, having at Rome's order been dismissed from the Maryknoll order he has served for thirty years.

In his just published book, *My Journey from Silence to Solidarity*, Roy tells his story, and he is on tour speaking to standing room only crowds of like believers. What I experienced at the reformed church on Sunday was a lesson for me about how the lights can be turned off on your hopes, your dreams, your beliefs. Roy has known his own agony in the garden, personally, emotionally, physically, spiritually, he has lived his agony, breathed it in and survived a broken heart and is walking through darkness into the light of truth.

So I've said that my life is a prayer of gratitude, and it is. I always go back (way back) to lessons of my childbearing years. I recall that first labor room nurse in 1958 to whom I spoke in my 11th hour of physical agony, my 20-year-old innocent truth, *"I don't think I can go through with this!"*, and then her harsh yet truthful response to me, *"It's a little late to think about that, honey."* I walked the agony, and it ended with the most beautiful ecstasy – the gift of my first born child asleep in my arms.

Emotional stress has been too real for me over decades – talk about going through the darkness. But in reminding myself always of my gift of faith, the all loving God I call Mystery of Life, I come to a reaching out and a reaching in -- out to the other kindred souls who walk with me, and in -- to my inner self – to where my soul rests, where my true God exists. The emotional journey for me may be dark and frightening at times. That's been my history and may again be. But I know this: my journey, my life is a gift, a gift of gratitude. Darkness may come into my journey, but remember, the journey is the way. I will experience the light again. I feel it right now.

❧ ❧ ❧

"This is wonderful, Mom, *wonderful*."

We were rushed for time as Mom had an appointment with her psychologist and I had a meeting at the Arts Center of the Capital Region on River Street to pitch a new idea I have for a class called The Writer's Circle, so I quickly read:

cmp, 2-18-13

"Right Work"

I know this to be true:

Your first work is to find your gift.

Your second work is to give it.

By work I don't mean a job or a career, I mean one's "*right work*," one's talent, the gift we are meant to open and share with others. We may or may not get paid for it.

It took me nearly 20 years to find my right work, but when I did, I was filled with such an immediate sense of *joy*, light, happiness, *love*, that I knew my life was forever changed. I woke up propelled forward with a powerful inner certainty and confidence that these shoes fit and would lead the way if I put them on.

While I was lucky enough to have interesting, well-compensated work from the time I graduated from The College of Saint Rose in 1980, first with the State of Connecticut; then with Maher, Pastor & Stevens, a Hartford, CT based advertising and public relations company, where I handled PR for The Connecticut State Lottery; next with The Sage Colleges, first as a publicist, soon Director of Communications; then founder/owner of Books Worth Writing, publisher of *The Remembering Book*; then a communications consultant and adjunct instructor at Russell Sage, where I loved teaching Public Speaking... it wasn't until almost two decades later, the fall of 1999, and I can pinpoint the exact "firefly moment" here, that I found my true life's work.

It was September 4, 1999, Labor Day, the morning of my son Christopher's 10th birthday. I was jogging around Walden's Pond (love that name) in Guilderland when all of a sudden *wooosh*...a story began playing in my mind. A young boy (not Chris) is waking up and it's his birthday and he smells chocolate cake baking and the doorbell rings and it's his grandmother who always gives him the best present every year and she hands him this big silver box... I could hear them talking and feel their feelings.

Racing home, I ran to my keyboard, heart pounding, sweating, and typed it all out in a flourish. I printed out those five pages and hugged them. "This is a book," I said, crying I was so happy. It was like I'd been searching for something my whole life, without even realizing it, and then *BOOM*, I had found it.

My first work was accomplished.

The second work, the finding a way to give my gift, was not for the faint of heart. It took nearly two years of daily effort, trial and error, writing, editing, revising, research and networking and craft-building and rejections, 179 "no" letters to be exact, before my first book was published. It was a long, hard road, but here's the good news: when you find your purpose in life, it comes with an arsenal of support. You are like a magnet drawing toward you everything and everyone you need to move forward.

I always tell my sons that I don't care what work you do in the world, just find something you *love*. When you find your right work, work that you are passionate about, work doesn't feel like work at all. Work feels like joy.

⁂ ⁂ ⁂

About an hour later, I popped in to Market Block Books to chat with my friend, Manager Stanley Hadsell, and there was my Mom, looking for an "inspirational" book to bring to her friend, Joannie, who was back in the psychiatric unit at Samaritan Hospital.

"How did your doctor's appointment go, Mom?" I asked.

"Dr. Van Dyne said he sees a real change in me," she said, her face bright and happy. "He says the writing is working."

⁂ ⁂ ⁂ ⁂ ⁂

Week 13, February 28, 2013

Beloved Pets – Woman Can (1/4 way there ☺)

We met for an early dinner at The Ale House on River Street as it was near the Missing Link Church where we intended to attend a community rally called to discuss quality of life issues in the North Central section of Troy. The burning topic of the moment is the murder of a young man who was lured to Corliss Park apartments by two teenage girls, 16 and 18, via an internet offer of sex, then confronted by four teenage boys and stabbed to death, all for the less than $40 in his wallet.

I live up the hill from North Central. I want to join in tonight to listen and see how I can be a better neighbor. I am bringing my Sunny books and *BIG* as gifts.

Mom ordered a turkey Reuben; me, grilled chicken atop a dinner salad. I told Mom I'd just discovered "Front Parlor Storytellers" which meets here at the Ale House under the direction of Abby Lublin. I went alone and was glad when writer friend Amy Halloran invited me to join her table. The topic that night was "Troy." I felt so at home.

"This place is like Marty Burke's," Mom said, referring to the landmark pub in South Troy, an institution for generations, now sadly soon set to close. I read first:

cmp, 2-25-13

Beloved Pets

Despite being bitten on the lips by the too-friendly dog of a friend of my father's one summer night at our camp on Burden Lake, and the Emergency Room nightmare that followed, as a child I always wanted a dog. My father always refused.

One Christmas I wrote a play about two kids who find a stray dog on a snowy night and "their father let's them keep it!" My sister, Nor, and brother, Michael, were stellar in the lead roles, and the Freihofer's holiday cookies I bought at Mrs. Milos's store were tasty, and the audience, Mom, Dad, Nana, and Uncle Mark gave a standing ovation but, alas, the answer was still "no pets."

Then, one October day, "Frisky" arrived in the mail. My sweet Aunt Bett Phoenix, living in San Francisco at the time, sent him as a birthday present. When I read the card and realized it was *a real live turtle*, I nearly burst with excitement. I opened the box and let the little creature slide out onto the kitchen table.

All of 2 inches long huddled beneath its shell, the turtle didn't move. Was he frozen or freeze-dried? I didn't know how turtles traveled. "Hey little guy," I said, gently stroking his shell with my finger. "It's okay." I waited and waited. I feared he was dead. I named him "Frisky" for his hometown. "Come on out, Frisky," I coached.

Finally, four tiny scaly feet stretched out, then a pointy tail, then a head. One foot moved and then another. Frisky was defrosted. I was in love.

Mom took me to buy turtle food and a plastic house with a swimming pool, palm tree, and cabana. Dad said Frisky could stay as long as I kept him "out of sight."

Frisky was a good and faithful pet. When he reached his demise, Mike, Nor and I gave him a proper funeral in a Cracker Jacks box coffin, then buried him behind the shed.

Fast forward nearly three pet-less decades....

My son, Chris, wanted a dog so badly, but settled for a guinea pig named "Skippy." Chris built Skip an elaborately constructed running maze made of Legos. After Skippy died, we had a short run with a Golden Retriever puppy named "Champ" who unfortunately had a biting problem and we had to find him a better placement.

Meanwhile, middle son, Connor, kept begging for a cat. Tony always said "no." Finally, on his 10th birthday when Connor pleaded, "Mom, please, *all I really want* is a cat," something snapped inside. "Okay, let's go," I said. We drove straight to get one.

"Boots," a black tuxedo cat with white paws, was a dear heart. Even Tony fell in love. We were officially "cat people." All five of us were heartbroken when Boots went out for an adventure and never returned. We adopted two more cats, first "Penny," and then "Bandit," who are still happily running the house in Guilderland.

After Tony and I separated and I bought this house in Troy, I adopted a fat orange Garfield-look-alike named "Junior." Junior kept me company on many a tear-filled day, always listening really well and not saying anything stupid.

Two years later, youngest son, Dylan, and his friends brought home a tiny stray kitten they'd found in Frear Park. They called it "Bro" like they call each other, and I got talked into keeping the little tabby with a coat as soft as mink. At the vet's we discovered "Bro" was a "Sis," but it was too late to change her name.

Unfortunately Junior *really hated* having a new cat in the house and after a few escapes and retrievals (we'd get calls from neighbors and the Park Pub saying "Junior's here") -- one day left and never came back. We're convinced Junior's found a new home where she can be the top-dog cat.

I still dream of having a dog. A few months ago, Columbus and I bought an adorable Yellow Lab puppy from a breeder. I named her "Casey," my Nana's maiden name, and the name I wanted to give a daughter if I had one (Casey or Grace). A few weeks in, though, it became apparent that training a Lab puppy was a full-time job and we agreed to wait until we are living together and could shoulder this responsibility equally. We found a loving family for Casey. I cried like a baby when she left.

As I write this morning, a new, as-yet-unnamed cat is curled up sleeping next to Dylan downstairs. We thought it would be nice for Bro to have a buddy.

This pretty black 1-yr-old girl was not properly cared for. She was pregnant, but so mal-nourished her fetuses weren't viable. She was spayed the day before we adopted her from the Hudson Mohawk Humane Society. She is exhausted, barely able to eat – but you can see in her eyes how much she already loves us and I can see how much Dylan already loves her. It's a frosty February morning outside, but toasty warm in here.

* * *

"Oh, this is really good, Col," Mom said. Then she shook her head. "I don't know," she said, taking out her papers. "Mine might be too deep."

"Do you think mine's too shallow?" I said, always defensive about my writing.

"That's not what I meant, Col." Then she read:

psm 2-27-13

"Woman Can"

Now that I have time in my life to think, to read, to watch a 3-hr. PBS documentary on the achievements of American women, time to write, to compose a piece of my own history, well, for me, all of that is called -- being retired.

My own perspective at 75 is first of all a grateful recognition that I still have a working mind. I'd like to ponder where my own time line has played out, as woman, through the decades of the fifties, sixties, seventies, eighties, nineties, into the new century, (do we say the zeroes?) and now the tens. For woman, from the pill to the present, things have changed. You might even say woman's world has been revolutionized. And I've been around to experience these changes. So while my right hand can still practice my Palmer Method, I will write.

In the PBS documentary I was reminded of the countless women who have told their stories and thus changed our lives -- women like Betty Friedan who gave us *The Feminine Mystique*; like Anita Hill, who revealed on national television her humiliating stories of her harassment ala Clarence Thomas. I will try to tell my story; I need to do that, because no one else can.

My little story is just that and can't compare to Betty, to Anita, or Eleanor Roosevelt or Hillary Clinton or Gloria Steinem or Rosa Parks or a hundred other sisters remembered on the documentary. I am indebted to these modern pioneers of women's liberation and equal rights. These are the women who have made it beneficial and possible, indeed made it necessary -- a requirement, that we each tell our own story.

Here I'll say I always try to avoid overused by definition clichés. One cliché says

that actions speak louder than words. But the hospital visit I had with a friend of mine this past week tells part of my story -- because I didn't just think about doing it -- I did it. I met my very special friend Joannie two years ago when we were patients together in the

Geri-psych ward. We both deal with our mental health issues, and my friend's issues have challenged her repeatedly and she's been back in the hospital several times since we met. We have built our relationship by talking on the phone usually 2 or 3 times a week. Joannie is close to seventy, lives alone in a nearby city on subsidized housing, on public assistance, receiving Meals on Wheels, food stamps, depending on public transportation, and most hurting to her she is without a close family, and has few friends.

I consider it a gift to me that even though we don't see each other in person our relationship has grown into a friendship. To sit together and have a personal visit, woman to woman, this is a powerful story worth telling. In this hospital experience I know and feel and drink in a cup of love, pouring over and soothing, and comforting a hurting heart. I've made it over to the hospital twice to see my friend. We talk about our lives, about taking one day at a time, about how God and Mary and the saints and angels love us and are here for us. Our words are not all preachy, we've covered the Oscars, the good news, bad news, and how her day goes.

I was able to give Joannie a beautifully illustrated book on the 23rd Psalm which she loves. And the one-day-at-a-time wisdom helps her as well because my friend doesn't know if she'll even be allowed to go back to her apartment. She waits to learn what her next move will be; perhaps it will mean moving into assisted living. The uncertainty frightens her.

The two words that came to me after watching the 3-hour documentary on all those courageous women are the same words I chose for this writing: Woman Can. These are the encouraging words Joannie needed to hear, and she needed to hear them in person from another woman who calls her friend. They are saving words for me as well. I read the sign that says Woman Can and it points to those actions that authenticate, validate, and bring life to my own life. The action and the word; for me you can't have one without the other. Thus energized, I take pen in hand and construct (note the action verb *construct*) in my still-trying to be perfect Palmer Method those words that speak my truth. It's why I call my writing My Labor of Love (note the action word *labor.)*

For me, a woman trying to heal herself, the words speak loud and clear and indeed become the action. The action to get myself to the hospital so I could share a word with my friend Joannie shows me that indeed the action happens so that the words can happen. So this co-mingling, this marriage if you will between action and word makes my life a win-win experience. It just proves to me -- and I better believe it -- let me say it again and don't you forget it, Peg: **Woman Can**

* * *

"Wow, Mom," I said. "Wow!"

We hurried off to the meeting at the Missing Link, then on to the Arts Center of the Capital Region to hear two writers, Margaret Roach (sister of my beautiful writer friend, Marion Roach Smith) and Katrina Kenison read from and discuss their latest books.

It was a full and inspiring (albeit a bit exhausting) evening.

* * * * *

Week 14, March 7, 2013

My Gift of Faith – Neighbors

We met for tea at my house, sitting at the kitchen table by the sliding-glass door looking out at my small backyard with the one oak tree, rope swing hanging down, and the wide open expanse of Frear Park beyond. That view is what sold me on this house.

"Meet Sneak," I said, as our newly adopted black cat scooted past.

"*Sneak*?" Mom said, laughing.

"Dylan named her," I said. "The day after we brought her home she snuck off and hid behind the furnace and we couldn't find her for hours. And she keeps finding new hiding places. Dyl said if I didn't like the name Sneak (I didn't) I could pretend it was Sneakers and that Sneak was her nickname."

Mom laughed again. "I love that boy."

We talked about family, my work, how Mom's psychiatrist lowered the dosage of one of her depression medications (the one making her feel so tired) and how both he and her psychologist agree "the writing is a really good thing." *Hooray!*

We talked about plans for Easter.

"I am so heartbroken about my church," Mom said. Then she read:

psm 3-7-13

My Gift of Faith

I made a commitment to my daughter and I'll give her credit for setting me on a positive path; working in, over, around and through my depression. Today my topic is Faith, and that's Faith with a capital F. I say that because it is my gift of Faith alone which has saved me. Faith is the ever-presence in my human experience, something sacred beyond my ability to comprehend, or control, or manipulate, or lie to or ignore. Faith is a gift from a Loving God.

By faith I am not referring to my Roman Catholic religion. At birth it was my parents who determined that I would be Roman Catholic and I have held to that religion for all of my 75 years. While I am still a Roman Catholic by choice, much has changed and I suffer with heartache, sadness, and disappointment and I need to make a distinction between what Rome is saying and doing and what my Faith means to me.

I've gone way beyond those years of innocence when my Faith and my religion were one and the same. Now in these times when I so disagree with so much of what my church is saying and doing, and I might otherwise just walk away, it is my Gift of Faith that comforts me and assures me that all is not lost. I can't begin to explain it, but I know -- even in my unknowing -- that God is present and will not fail me. That presence is my gift of Faith.

There are many times when I have felt my Faith lifting me out of darkness. I recall a happening, maybe it was twenty years ago, when I was an in-patient struggling with mental issues. I was slowly walking around the psych ward, staring up at the framed pictures on the walls, contemplating how I could end my misery. I was in the throes of depression, near despair and wanting my life to be over.

I remember going back into my room and like a child, almost in a trance, I knelt down beside the bed and for the first time in my life a feeling came over me and it was telling me that *there was no God*. That for me was the height of despair and I nearly panicked. I remember praying something like, "Oh God, my mind tells me you do not exist. If you do exist, please help me."

That was my gift of faith; when God heard my un-prayer and made it a prayer.

So what is my Gift of Faith? For me, it is:

- A knowing without knowing
- A believing when belief is shattered
- A seeing when I walk in darkness
- And, in a terrifying silence, hearing "Fear not."

I know a Faith that promises me – and never breaks that promise – that there is a God who is always with me; sends angels to comfort me, teachers to teach me, and prophets to guide me. I can keep trying because there's one thing I know for certain – my Faith will not fail me.

I'm always looking for the words to explain what I'm trying to say and I'm always falling short. Nothing new here. But if I ask myself what it is that remains when everything falls short, my answer is, truly, my Gift. My Gift of Faith remains.

* * *

"This is amazing, Mom. So powerful. Thank you." Then I read this:

cmp, 3-5-13

Neighbors

When Tony and I married in 1980, we moved to South Windsor, Connecticut, into a beautiful suburban apartment complex with indoor and outdoor pools and tennis courts. We were both so busy -- Tony in sales with the Personal Products Division of Johnson & Johnson (our end tables were sanitary napkin cartons) -- me job-hunting all day then cooking Betty Crocker at night -- the thought of meeting neighbors didn't cross my mind.

Within the year, wanting to save money for a house, we moved to a much cheaper apartment in Hartford, close to my new job with the State of Connecticut Energy Office and to Trinity College where I had enrolled in a master's program, evenings. I still recall the United Nations onslaught of cooking smells entering that apartment building after work, the exhaust fumes and screech-rumble of brakes from the bus depot outside our bedroom window, and how we snuck a contraband live Christmas tree up the elevator to the 6th floor, but I cannot recall meeting a single neighbor.

Was it youth? We were in our very early 20s. Our ambitious focus on work? Were we too wrapped up in "us" to care about anybody else?

Saving money like misers, we bought our first house a year later, a small ranch on a country road, with a working fireplace and an old in-ground pool in the backyard. A row of tall pine trees bordered the pool and shedding green needles made the water a nightmare to clean. I think we swam in it once. The frogs loved it though. Our only nearby neighbor was a few donuts short of a dozen. His "hobby" was shooting birds in his backyard -- not clay birds, real ones. Needless to say we never hung out.

Soon Tony was offered a promotion and we moved back to the Capital District, renting an apartment as we looked for a new house. The day I saw that white colonial with black shutters on Tudor Road in Albany, I fell in love. I walked to the kitchen, then out to the yard. I imagined a garden, children playing. This felt like home. We made an offer and bought this treasure, not knowing the *real treasure* would be the neighbors.

Judy and Keith Reynolds "next door" hosted a potluck dinner and all the families on the street came to welcome us. Years later, Judy and

Keith hosted our baby shower. When 2-year-old Chris visited our other next-door neighbors, Addie and Lew Muhlfelder, they showed him the dish of gum drops that would "always be there" for him. When 3-yr-old Chris started a business, loading up his wagon with old *Times Union* newspapers and heading up the street to sell them, the Muhlfelders bought them all.

On Tudor Road we had a block party every summer, checked in on each other after storms and surgeries, celebrated babies, birthdays, graduations, offered comfort in times of grief. I learned what it meant to be a good neighbor. I met my new best friend.

When, after a decade in that neighborhood, me pregnant with our third son, Tony insisted we move to suburbia for "better schools," I laid down on the floor and cried. I argued that the Albany schools would be fine, but Tony also had a dream of building a house and in a marriage you have to care about your partner's dreams, too.

I insisted on postponing the move until I brought new baby, Dylan, home to 6 Tudor Road. I wanted to see the balloons on the lamppost and have my neighbors visit.

The neighborhood gave us a farewell party. A well-intentioned, but painful gift was a framed photograph of all the children on the street. A week later, I sat on our front steps, 4-yr-old Chris on one side, 1-yr-old Connor on the other, infant Dylan snuggled in my arms as two long moving vans arrived. I sobbed like someone had died.

The new neighborhood, Blockhouse Creek Court in Guilderland, was great, too. Our boys played in the grassy circle at the center of the cul-de-sac and rode bikes around it with the Shamlian kids. They managed lemonade stands in the summer, trick-or-treated, went sledding on "Lois and Jon's hill," explored the creek behind our house.

In August of 2008, after fourteen years in that home, as Tony and I separated, a small moving truck came for my boxes of books, my clothes, some dishes, and my office desk and chair, and I moved to this house on Park Boulevard in Troy.

I don't recall my new neighbors coming to welcome me. I was so emotionally distraught, though, and exhausted attempting to furnish the house in two weeks time before my boys came back from vacation with their father, I probably scared them off.

Little by little, though, greetings were exchanged. Mary Jaffarian from across the street called. There was a garter snake in her garage. "Could one of your boys help?" The next day she brought us homemade chocolate-chip cookies. Neighbor Joan kept a spare key for me. Neighbor Sarah came to a bookstore signing of mine and stayed for hours to help. Neighbor Kari helped with tax assessment stuff.

Park Boulevard is a street in transition. Just in the past six months, three new families moved in. I kept intending to stop by. Finally, last Sunday, I made a simple batch of brownies, divided them onto three plastic plates, wrote out three "Welcome to the Neighborhood" cards, and set off to welcome my new neighbors.

Two nights later, I was hosting my writer's group when my doorbell rang. New neighbor Alicia was locked out of her house. As she waited for the locksmith, I invited her to join in our discussion and stay for dinner. The next day she came over with a bottle of wine and a card, "Good neighbors are a blessing."

Week 15, March 15, 2013

New Pope Hope – My Mother's Garden

We met for lunch at the Hungry Fish Café on Pawling Avenue after reading how the owner, Sarah Fish, was committed to using locally grown ingredients. The atmosphere was fun; the food was delicious. We talked about the new pope.

"That's what I wrote about," Mom said, then read:

psm, 3-14-13

Pope Francis We Hope

I'm almost glad Col and I agreed we'd make these writings not too long, just a few pages, because I need a start/stop ruler for writing about the new pope. It all happened so quickly, like fast forward. Within a brief two weeks, Pope Benedict announces he will step down, citing age and exhaustion. The cardinals are called to Rome for the conclave (a word I learn comes from the Latin "with key") suggesting secret, silent and sequestered. Then comes the chimney black smoke white smoke drama and before we know it we have Pope Francis I. A lot to digest and of course I had been glued to MSNBC in my apartment or listening to the radio in my car. Then in the time it took me to stop into Friendly's for lunch, I came out, turned the car radio on and heard, just like that, "We have a Pope!"

This is big for me and I do want to be brief – and positive – short and sweet-- quite a challenge. So here comes the prayer I'm clinging to – it's called Hope.

Maybe God is giving my church another chance -- to repent, repair and reform -- forgiveness for all the sins and scandals, sexual abuse of children, cover-up by the clergy, the bishops, the very cardinals who have come to Rome and now have chosen the man who will replace Benedict. I've grown so critical and cynical, felt so personally violated; ashamed to admit I'm Roman Catholic. In this penitential season of Lent, I think of a Jesus who suffered, who would be denied even betrayed by those he called friends and disciples. What would Jesus think or say about all the sins and scandal?

Well, here comes Francis, and we quickly learn he is not a Vatican bureaucrat. In fact he's the first ever pope from the Western Hemisphere, from Argentina. He shuns

all the pomp and pageantry of the papal monarchy; he lives and works for and with the poor. No limousines, he uses public transportation, rides a bicycle, or walks. We're told at the Holy Thursday ritual of washing the feet of his followers, Francis has knelt and washed the feet of people afflicted with AIDS. What we see and learn is that Francis is a humble, holy man of God; considers himself a servant. And I am a Catholic who has been Catholic all my life and I'm still searching for the answers that will align me with the man of Nazareth who came with a message that was all about the power of love.

Then back to the media I learn something else. This very same man, Francis, who has dedicated his life giving hope and service to the poor is the same man who has loudly condemned the very reforms being called for by Catholic progressives like myself, i.e., the ordination of women, a married clergy, gay rights. In fact, the Catholic woman president of Argentina has championed the right of gays to marry and this is now the law of the land. Pope Francis says she is all wrong, even sinful. You can see why this topic of a new pope peels back for me all the layers of assumptions about what my faith has been and is saying to me, what my church has to teach me.

So I knew I had to write something about the new pope – this is big – certainly for me because I do care. I want to stay Catholic -- but will I be able to do that and remain true to my conscience, true to what Jesus is asking of me? This thing called hope is one of the gifts of my faith. Let me celebrate the gifts I have received from a loving God and just keep it simple and straight in this milieu of challenging choices. I'm celebrating and I'm walking the walk just as I keep talking my talk. Jesus, what do you think? What would you do? What would you say? Where are You, Jesus? That's where I want to be.

* * *

We chatted for a bit, and then I read:

cmp, 3-8-13

My Mother's Garden

"In search of my mother's garden, I found my own."
Alice Walker

When I read *The Color Purple*, by Alice Walker, in 1982, the book shook me to the core. I circled lines like: "I'm pore, I'm black, I may be ugly......but I'm here." And.... "I think it pisses God off if you walk by the color purple in a field somewhere and don't notice it." I sought out everything I could find by this author. The day I read Walker's essay, "In Search of Our Mother's Gardens," first published in *Ms.* magazine in 1974, this sentence made me cry:

"Our mothers and grandmothers have, more often than not anonymously, handed on the creative spark, the seed of the flower they themselves never hoped to see."

I thought, of course, of my own mother. How she handed on the "sparks" of reading and writing to me. How she labored and sacrificed so greatly to raise us six children, instilling a fierce respect for education in all of us, while never having the time or money to pursue her own dream of a college degree. I wonder... maybe after we finish writing this book, we could look into college programs for Mom. Russell Sage is right down the hill. I would help in any way possible. My mother is the wisest person I know. She should be awarded honorary doctoral degrees in faith, hope and charity, for starters.

Inspired by Alice Walker, I moved on to read the work of other celebrated African-American women authors, notably Maya Angelou and Toni Morrison. I soaked in the rich language, rhythm, and texture; I fell in love with the voices still in me today.

When it came time to chose a graduate thesis topic, I excitedly proposed "Manifestations of Creativity in the Works of Alice Walker" (or some such title) - about how people without pen or paper, paint or brush, still found outlets for their art -- in quilts, in gardens, in the patterns they swept in the dirt outside. Because of the heavily patriarchal-Anglo-Saxon focus of "the canon" in college literature departments of the time, it was hard to find a "second reader," (two professors must approve a thesis). I persevered, though, and *wrote what my heart called me to write*. Mom taught me that.

I am a writer today because of her. Every time a kid in a school asks: "who inspired you to be a writer?" I say, "My mother." I tell them how some nights I would wake up after she'd come home from working the 4 to 11pm shift at William's Press in Menands and I'd peek around the avocado-colored refrigerator to watch her sitting at the kitchen table, her hand moving in a swift cursive swirl across the paper and how she had such a look of joy on her face. I wanted that. I wanted to be where she was.

Did my Mom dream of being an author…seeing a book with her name on the cover? Maybe. Regardless, it is a dream I have *for* her – a dream we will see realized.

⁂ ⁂ ⁂

We had both brought books to recommend: me, *Looking for Signs*, by my author friend Diane Cameron; Mom, *The Four Agreements*, by Don Miguel Ruiz. She had also just finished Sonya Sotomayor's memoir, *My Beloved World*, and was half-way through Deepak Choprah's new *Super Brain*.

"I'm addicted to books," Mom said. We laughed.

"*Addicted to books*….I love that," I said. "Me, too."

As we finished our coffee and complimentary apple cake, I told Mom how our bookseller friend Stanley had been good enough to read our manuscript (to date) and was insistent that we reach out to Oprah. "There was something in the way Stanley spoke, Mom, it was as if it was an angel speaking, if you believe in angels."

"Oh yes, I do," Mom said, assuredly. "Absolutely."

⁂ ⁂ ⁂ ⁂ ⁂

Spring

Week 16, March 22, 2013

Perennials – My Tax Angel

Seated in a booth at the Plum Blossom restaurant on Hoosick Street, where my brother, Dan, once worked, we ordered sweet and sour chicken, vegetable spring rolls and chicken satay. I poured the tea.

My mother looked completely out of it – withdrawn, sad, joyless. I started to ask "how are you doing," but stopped and tried something new. "So what's good?" I said.

My mother locked eyes with me. She huffed, annoyed, and shook her head.

"I know you don't want to hear how I'm really doing, which is *awful*."

"You're right, Mom. I don't." I didn't want to be mean, but I think every time Mom talks about how depressed she is, she gives the depression more power. I'm hoping if she thinks about what's *good*, instead of what's bad, she'll feel better.

I shared how Dylan and Columbus and I went to hear a band at The Irish Mist in South Troy for St. Patrick's Day. "They did *Danny Boy* and *When Irish Eyes are Smiling*. You would have loved it, Mom. You'll have to come with us next year."

After lunch, I read first:

cmp, 3-20-13

Perennials

It's the first day of spring and I smile knowing that the daffodil bulbs hibernating beneath the snow around the one big tree in my backyard will soon send up green shoots, then sweet-smelling frilly yellow flowers.

When I was a little, I loved dandelions, baby suns rising out of city sidewalks. "A dandelion is a powerful flower," my girl Sunny says. "There's a *lion* right in its name."

During summers at our family's camp on Burden Lake where at last, *at last,* I could ride my bike with abandon down the dirt road to the beach, or across the dike to Kay's Pizza, on my return I'd stop and pick wildflowers – daisies, asters, blue cornflowers, purple thistles, black-eyed Susans, Queen Anne's Lace, burnt orange and red "Indian paint brushes," as my mother called them, to arrange in a jelly jar.

Each Easter, my father bought fancy florist corsages for my mother, Noreen, and me to wear on our new outfits to Mass (a tradition I loved when I was 6 and loathed when I was 16.) My Uncle Mark always bought my Mom a beautiful Easter Lilly.

In the center of the steep lawn beside our house on High Street, beneath a white latticed arbor, there resided a tall statue of the Blessed Mother, surrounded by rose bushes. The day I got married, at 21, the photographer took a photo of me there.

In May the lilac trees at the edge of our property filled the air with perfume. There were fragrant Lilies of the Valley and purple violets everywhere. My Nana had a long "flower box" in her yard which she filled with annuals: yellow and purple faced pansies in the spring, pink and white petunias and golden marigolds in the summer.

As an adult, I learned about perennials. I loved the notion of planting flowers that would bloom again and again for years. There was something so hopeful in that.

I planted my first small perennial garden in the backyard of our house on Tudor Road, mostly Shasta Daisies and Rudbeckia (black-eyed Susans) perhaps because they reminded me of the wild ones I picked as a child. In the front yard I planted dozens and dozens of tulip bulbs – red, yellow, orange, purple, pink. Albany, in honor of its Dutch heritage, hosts a Tulip Festival in Washington Park each May and crowns a Tulip Queen.

When we moved to Guilderland, I planted a very ambitious perennial garden with a stepping-stone path and bird baths -- more daisies and black-eyed Susans, Lilacs, old-fashioned Bleeding Hearts, primroses, English Lavender, Dianthus, Gaillardia, bright yellow

Coreopsis, Purple Echinacea, Mums. My boys loved spotting the butterflies and hummingbirds hovering about the gorgeous-smelling purple Buddleia, "butterfly bush."

On the day they were baptized into the Catholic Church, I planted a yellow forsythia bush for each of them and gave a matching one to their godparents.

That garden provided us with countless bouquets from late March through November, the lavender sometimes lasting through the winter.

I also cleared a long walking trail, by hand like a pioneer, along the back of our property. Driving out to country roads, I dug up orange daylilies (my father loved them), daisies, thistles, and other wildflowers and transplanted them to the borders of the trail. I planted gorgeous-smelling "Stargazer Lilly" bulbs. I hauled in a bench so my boys and I could sit and see the creek down below and enjoy the quiet nature around us.

The wildflowers did okay, but the Stargazers were a big mistake. They were a tasty salad bar for the deer that also liked our trail.

For fourteen years, I tended that garden and trail. I wept when I said good bye.

I have been in this new house in Troy for nearly five years and, except for the daffodils (one must always have daffodils), until now I haven't had the heart to plant flowers. This may seem silly, I'm crying as I write, but today, on this first day of a brand new spring, I have decided to plant a garden...and not just any garden...a *perennial* one.

This feels big to me. It means I'm setting down roots, this house is home. I can picture sitting in that Adirondack chair, looking out at the big green expanse, a book in my hands, a grandchild laughing, enjoying the oak tree swing.

I always dreamed of living in a "real town" where I could walk to the library, stores and restaurants where people knew your name. I created that fictionally in the town of Bramble in the Willa books. But in real life, I am no longer searching for some illusive perfect town. The grass is green right here in Troy. Soon there will be daffodils, then sunny yellow dandelions. I was born here. I have returned. I bloomed here once. I am blooming here again. The more I commit to *living fully* in this town, working here, serving here, spending my hard-earned money here, contributing my ideas and energy....I grow happier and more content.

Planting a perennial garden is a sign I am here to stay.

❧ ❧ ❧

"Oh, that's really beautiful, Col," Mom said. "I wrote about my tax angel."

"Great title," I said, laughing. Then my mother read:

psm, 3-21-13

My Tax Angel

I kept an appointment today with a lady who has done my taxes every year for well over 30 years. I drove to the same house, rang the same doorbell, and greeted the same beautiful woman who has listened to my financial story for three decades and who has assembled all my paperwork and completed my taxes.

Emanuela Castle is a strong, kind, very intelligent woman who has been there for me over 30 years. All those years when I earned a secretary's salary, and a brief couple of years when I was director at Joseph's House, went to work every day, supported myself, guided my children and myself through all those years of financial uncertainty. I worked hard and tried to hold it all together and there was someone I visited once a year with all my records, terms like W-2, 1040's tax deductibles, to itemize or not to itemize. God sent me an angel and she would understand everything I was as a responsible taxpayer in a free country and had I paid the amount I owed, how many deductions, who was in college, what about stocks, etc.

Emanuela and I liked each other, respected each other, trusted each other. I found her when I was at the telephone company being a good secretary/support person for intelligent professional writers in media relations. One of those bright men I supported knew this "very smart lady over in Troy who did taxes." Perfect, right in my home town, I thought, and so the connection was made.

I had done taxes for years, buying each year the revised J. K. Lasser instruction book, a lot to learn when my husband was in sales. The thing now with Emanuela is I could sit down, talk to her, tell her what had transpired in my life and how did it affect what I owed the government. Emanuela put it all together. She was so knowledgeable, kept up with the tax rules and regulations, knew what could help me. I could ask Emanuela anything and she had or would get the right answer and the right form. She is someone I have relied on and who has never disappointed me.

Before she retired, Emanuela was a school teacher who took it upon herself to become a tax preparer to supplement her income. Like me, she was a divorced Catholic woman with dependents and a house to care for. In our brief annual catch-up talks over all these years we have touched on all the soup to nuts of being Catholic, being mothers, working women, self supporting. While my time with Emanuela was always brief, she has never rushed me and I have respected the value of her time. More than 30 years have gone by and she has shared my stories of Coleen, Michael, Noreen, Jerry, Dan and Kevin and my stories of what has gone on with me, emotionally, spiritually, financially, all of it. And once a year we get to tell the government what is the bottom line.

Now in 2013 I no longer have tax questions, at least very few. But it's tax time again and I'm still asking Emanuela to do my taxes and she's still saying, "of course." And we'll see what next year brings. Emanuela remains a kind, gentle, respectful, intelligent good friend, still helping me get my tax thing done. So this week I drove to Emanuela's house. (Thank God I'm still able to drive and thank God she still lives in her same house). I rang her bell, she opened her door, I thought a silent prayer of gratitude – and hugged my angel.

* * *

"I love this, Mom," I said, "you actually made taxes sound good."

* * * * *

Week 17, March 29, 2013

"Dear Oprah" (1/3rd way there ☺)

We met for lunch at my house. I made tuna-salad sandwiches with curry, raisins, and tarragon, my special recipe, served with vegetable soup, and strawberries.

We had decided to both write letters to Oprah. I read first:

cmp, 3-26-13

Dear Oprah,

Thank you. Thank you for the decades of inspiration you have given me, first as Sofia in *The Color Purple*, then through your daily afternoon talk show, now through *O* magazine. You have been one of my greatest teachers. I pray this letter reaches you.

I am 54, recently divorced after a 28-year-marriage, the mother of three sons, ages 18, 20 and 23, and the author of 17 books. **You** are in my novel, *Sunny Holiday*. Nine-year-old Sunny and her Mom are writing a rainbow shaped book on the wall of their apartment called *Free All Year*, about all the good things they are grateful for like singing, dancing and dandelions. They hope to get it published and meet you.

Sunny says: "I would love to meet Oprah. *Hope-rah*. That's what she gives people. *Hope*." See page 56 of the enclosed copy.

In my "Willa books" series, inspired by my ½ million selling first novel, *The Wedding Planner's Daughter*, 12-year-old Willa is a staunch believer in "Community Rent" – how we each owe a portion of our time, talent, or treasure – a value instilled in her by her friend Sulamina Mum, the female minister of her non-denominational church. I picture *you* playing Mum in the movie, Oprah. Autographed book enclosed.

I am now writing a book with my mother; our working title is: *Writing Us Right*. Here's the pitch: Two writers, a novelist grieving the end of a 28-year-marriage, and her 75-year-old poet mother battling chronic depression, plot to "write themselves right," promising to meet weekly for a year to share pieces they've written about what's *good*.

We hope our journey will bring inspiration to others, too. There is great power in pen on paper, first pouring out pain, then planting seeds, writing ourselves forward.

I do hope you will read our book when it's published.

Thank you for your precious time. I hope you enjoy the Sunny and Willa books, and my new picture book, *BIG*. If anyone on the planet is teaching us how to be the "biggest YOU that YOU can be" – it is, most definitely, **you**.

With sincerest gratitude,
Coleen Murtagh Paratore

"Oh, Col, that's beautiful...just beautiful," Mom said, and then she read:

psm, 3-28-13

Dear Oprah,

My daughter and I are each writing a separate letter to you because we've been working together on an exciting work of love since December. We hope to see it published before the year is out and it's very important to us that you know what we're doing. I'm 75 years old, a mother of six and grandmother of eight and I am one of the more than a million "Seniors who love Oprah".

I live alone in a small one bedroom apartment in senior housing. Your OWN network comes into my world every day – thank you for bringing this medium of divine magic to us – thank you – it is a treasure in my life. By continuing your labor of love you are sending a little bit of heaven right into my living room and into the world. I tell everyone about my favorite of all your offerings -- and that is Soul Sunday.

I wish I could find the words to tell you how you have been the platform and the voice which enables us to see and hear the great spiritual masters. I'm a writer – that's a gift I'm still learning to honor and share with sisters and brothers with whom I walk this earth. I pray, I meditate, I write it down. For example, here is a thought that came into my mind when I was watching Soul Sunday recently. It's a simple message and it came to me and I wrote it down: "Oprah opens the heavens and love angels fly down."

Thanks to you I've been able through my dark times and good times, in sickness and in health, to experience so many spiritual masters and other great minds. I call them Prophets in my Living Room. At 75 my memory challenges me (I've had shock therapy) but names like Eckhart Tolle, Deepak Chopra, Maya Angelou, Tony Morrison, Tony Robbins come to mind and that's only a sprinkling. I am a compulsive reader, I have a pleasant speaking voice, I'm a good writer and poet and I have years of journals. My very first empty journal called a Nothing Book was a gift from Coleen in 1983 which she inscribed "To my mother, who has such a way with words."

Whoever I am, I am above all, a spiritual traveler, searching for the truth. Unlike my daughter I have not had any of my work published although people whose opinion I respect tell me I could.

Please know Oprah that my mental health history is a long standing diagnosis of severe clinical depression. Several times beginning in the 80's I have been an in patient both at Four Winds Psychiatric Hospital in Saratoga and on the psychiatric ward at Samaritan Hospital in Troy. During my darkest periods, I overdosed on Tylenol twice and took an overdose of antidepressants in 2011. I see my psychologist for therapy twice a month and my psychiatrist for antidepressant medications on a regular basis.

It was Coleen's inspiration last Thanksgiving that she and I should come together once a week having written something positive to share. Col felt it would help me fight my near crippling depression and at the same time would help her to heal both emotionally and spiritually from a painful divorce that was also impacting on the lives of her three teenage boys now college age young men. I said "No" enough times, but she kept asking and I finally said yes.

It is a commitment I am honoring even when it seems too much.

I'm always reading, as I know you are, and always more than one book at a time. Currently it's Sonia Sotomayor's *My Beloved World* and the other author I just met thanks to you -- Don Miguel Ruiz. I went to my local independent book store and bought two copies of *The Four Agreements*. One I mailed to my grandson, Ryan, on his 19th birthday. (He has recently gotten into quite a bit of trouble and is struggling and I wanted something to touch his heart.) So there I was, watching Soul Sunday and hearing you and Don Miguel send the word of a loving God across the airways into my living room. Later I flipped opened to page 131, wrote a long letter to Ryan and suggested he read the Prayers there: *"Please take a moment to close your eyes, open your heart, and feel all the love that comes from your heart."*

This letter I'm writing now using a favorite pen and my best cursive Palmer Method is a love letter to you, Oprah. Thank you for coming into my life all these years and for bringing God's messengers with you for me to see and hear and visit with on a daily basis. In a perfect world we would be sitting together and Coleen and I would be talking with the woman named Oprah, a true friend, who has spent her life seeking, finding and bringing her Truth -- which I see as the Word of the All Loving Mystery Who is God -- to an ever waiting, still hungering and forever grateful world.

* * * * *

Week 18, April 5, 2013

Dear Lord, Help – Spring

This week I reached out to my friend Barb Burg for advice on how to get a letter into Oprah's hands. Barb is a superstar in the PR field....former V.P. of Publicity at Random House now V.P. for Global

Communications for Reuters. If I might brag a bit, when Barb was a junior at Russell Sage in the 1980's she did an internship with me. I taught her how to write a press release and pitch a story. She was super smart, creative, funny, and uber-confident. I knew she'd be a *rock star* in the field.

Barb was adamant about not contacting Oprah until the book is finished.

"Col, write the best book you can," she said, "then once it's published and you've created some buzz, that's the time to reach out to Oprah. And don't just write about what's good. Tell about the bad, too. People will want to know."

"Oh, thank God," my mother said when I shared Barb's advice. "Now I can write about how I really feel which is *bad, bad, bad.*"

Mom and I met for lunch at Finnbar's Pub on Broadway. I'd read they were planning an event supporting families of children with autism and I wanted to contribute an autographed copy of my book, *BIG*, as a raffle prize. We had a table by a sunny window in the back room all to ourselves. Mom read first:

psm, 4-5-13

Dear Lord Help

I've prayed Come Oh Holy Spirit and then Lord Grant Me the Serenity -- it has been a down time – you could say every day wants to be a down time with this depression demon wanting to do me in. And lately it has been with me strong, pushing me away from concentrating on the positive. I just couldn't think of something positive. Then last night, my near despair prayers were answered. The Mystery of a Loving God and the Holy Spirit and my designated angels came to me across the phone lines as Col shared a conversation she'd had with a long time professional woman friend and colleague. What this very successful woman in the publishing world was suggesting is that in our Writing Us Right venture we should be careful to sometimes include the dark side of our lives. Readers care and are interested. As I listened to Col I thought, oh God maybe I can write about where I am right now. All through winter and into spring I've been striving to bring out the positive, and it really and truly has helped me. Col was right, it has been good. But this past week was quite emotionally scary, and I was driven to put something down about where I was at, and I wrote twice in my journal.

Sharing it here will help me lift this burden from my heart and resume my healing. And that's a positive.

<u>Wed. of Holy Week, March 27, 2013, 9:15 am</u>

Dear God, I'm in a frightening place – too close to giving up on myself – it's as if each curtain or shade on each window in this enclosed circular room is slowly moving down to closing – silent doom warning. God be with me – my demons have the power to destroy me and yet there is the voice of Hope – only silent if I silence it. If I destroy myself it will be because I let the demons win.

I will never desert you – behold I am with you always.

(Then 3 days later I wrote)

<u>Holy Saturday, March 30, 2013, 8:45 am</u>

My brain is overloaded with no hope, I want rest and there is no rest. Think of all the times – so so many when you felt at the edge – standing on the precipice – about to slip and fall -- down down to death. God I am where I was all those times when I felt in despair – this is Hell – this is what madness tastes like. Last night I took myself over to OLV (my church Our Lady of Victory) *to the Good Friday Passion: Hatred, Lust for power, all the human weaknesses playing out to effect through torture and death the Final Crucifixion and still a voice crying in the desert wilderness "Don't do it – Make way for the God of Right – the God who saves. God you are never the silent voice – You are endless hope. God is endless longing to hold me, to save me, to vanish and banish the demons. Evil knows that if I can't forgive myself evil has won. The truth will set you free. God, yes, you are ever here – in the battered Jesus offering the Ever Presence, the Truth will set you free. Come follow me.*

(Later 12:55pm) *2 calls -- my brother Jim and my cousin Mary.*

God help me to remember how You love me. When I look so close into the abyss – too real to handle – when I think I' m losing my grip.

How to fight when I feel beaten
God help me to help myself
Depression has the power to destroy
Take your focus off danger – loss of hope.
Move your focus on one step toward being saved.
Evil wins when believers lose faith.

(end of journal entries)

⁂ ⁂ ⁂

So for this week that's what I've done – shared a small piece of my dark side – and in so doing brought it back to the light -- myself back to a healthy place – a place where I can function again, and nurture my spiritual energy, and use my gifts, and keep Writing Us Right.

⁂ ⁂ ⁂

"This is wonderful, Mom. Barb was right." When it was my turn, I read:

cmp, 3-30-13

Spring

It was winter when we began writing this book. Now a new season has begun.

This morning I emailed my "Cape friends," all the people who've come into my life during my 30-year connection with this special place. Out of financial necessity, I must sell my house. I asked them to spread the word.

My ex-husband, Tony, and I first visited Cape Cod in the spring of 1981 with our new friends Susan and Bruce Carlson of West Hartford, CT We stayed at Susan's parents' The Rosania's home, in Wellfleet, and biked to the National Seashore for a chilly, but glorious picnic. From that moment on, Tony and I were hooked. We went to the Cape every summer, first staying at hotels, like The Queen Anne Inn in Chatham, then renting a house for a week each July in a best-kept-secret beach community called "Popponesset" that our Albany neighbors Joan and Tom Noonan told us about.

Our boys loved playing baseball each morning at the Community Center, swimming, digging and castle-building at the beach all afternoon, walking out along "The Spit," then heading up to "Poppy Marketplace" evenings for chowder, candy, and ice cream. We danced to the music of the bands that played in the courtyard there. The boys made "summer friends." Tony relaxed. I found a setting for my Willa books. We all went home with sand in our sneakers and memories to last a lifetime.

When a house in Popponesset came on the market in 2000 – our twentieth anniversary – Tony and I took a financial leap of faith and bought it. The owners were Gloria and Bill Malone. Gloria and I connected instantly – both Irish, mothers of three sons, attended churches named Christ the King. Gloria made tea and we chatted. I will never forget pushing aside the heavy gold drapes in the living room and gasping as I saw – *the Atlantic Ocean*-- down there at the end of the street. It was a dream come true.

(I had to stop reading here as I tried to hold back tears and regain composure. My Mom reached over and touched my hand. "Oh, Col.. I know how hard this is for you.")

Eight years later, as a non-negotiable condition of our separation, Tony insisted that I sign over that house to him. A year later, I bought a different Cape house, this one on the Moonakis River in East Falmouth, just two miles from the other house. Nearly an acre of land, a private dock, swans and ospreys gliding by, so peaceful and quiet. I named it While Away. I imagined it would be so convenient for our sons when they came to the Cape each summer to visit both their Dad and me, someday with our grandchildren.

After sending the email to my Cape friends this morning, I sat at my computer and sobbed. Then I suited up and went for a run. It was warm, a bright blue sky, children swinging in the park, a couple playing tennis. Spring. I saw that the trail by the pond had been freshly cleared and so, *YAY*, for the first time this season, I turned right and ran along the water then left up into the woods where there is a waterfall...*a waterfall* hidden from view...then up around the golf course and down the hill home.

There, in my sunny front yard, the clump of crocuses planted by the former owner had all opened and bloomed in unison, a purple cloaked chorus singing. Happy Spring.

Later there were kind emails from Cape friends.... Carol Chittenden of Eight Cousins bookstore, Paul Rifkin of the Moonakis Restaurant, author buddy Kate Feiffer on Martha's Vineyard and many others. I may never own a home "on Cape" again, but I will always have friends there and memories to last a lifetime.

One season ends, a new one begins... *spring...spring...spring.*

Week 19, April 11, 2013

Signs – School Days, School Days

We planned to meet for lunch at the Knotty Pine on 15th Street, one of our favorite old Troy spots. Mom was late, quite odd for her. She's usually always early. When she finally arrived, she looked awful. She'd gained weight; her face was expressionless. When she saw me there waiting for her in a booth by the window, she didn't smile.

I talked about all the drama in my life right now. I talked and talked, Mom ate and ate. She stood up quickly and rushed the bathroom. She was gone a long time.

"It's all the junk food I'm eating," Mom said. "All the stuff that's bad for me." She took out some pages. "I started writing about teachers.

How they've been so important to me my whole life, but I didn't have time to finish."

"No worries, Mom. Email it to me and I'll add it in." And then I read:

cmp, 4-12-13

Signs

I'm a big believer in signs. Every morning when I go for a run, about three miles, except for Sunday, no matter the weather except for ice, I keep my eyes open for them. Signs from Spirit, answers, clues on next steps in my life, mostly my writing life.

For two years now I've been working on a novel drawn loosely from what happened to me on the night of my sixteenth birthday. The working title was The Pink Sweater, a sequel to my autobiographical novel, *Dreamsleeves*, also set in 1970's Troy. Then, during a Highlights Foundation writer's retreat, I got the idea to revise the story, so that it could be any girl, any town, any time. I spent the next six months revising.

It was stronger, but still not right. When my passion turned to this new book I'm writing with Mom, I moved the seed basket labeled "pink sweater" off my desk.

Then, just this past week, out running, I saw three signs: first a pink hair "scrunchie," the next day a pink glove; two days later a long pink ribbon.

I brought them home and set them on top of the The Pink Sweater seed basket.

Yesterday morning, Columbus called just as I was beginning to write. He began singing to me as he often does. Generally I keep on writing, but today I closed my eyes and listened appreciatively.

"I love you, Babe," I said.

"Love you, more," he said.

When we hung up I typed a new first line:

"I am not the kind of girl who wears the color pink, but when I heard that boy singing that song, I thought maybe I might give it a try."

That was yesterday. Today I am already five chapters into writing what feels like, finally, the book I've been wanting to write all along.

It's important to pay attention to signs... and to listen to love songs.

* * *

A few days later, my Mom sent me her piece about teachers. As I read it, I was sad that I didn't get to hear it in her own beautiful voice. When our book is published, I hope this is a chapter she'll choose to read aloud at one of our signing events.

psm, 4-10-13

School Days School Days

Teachers have guided my long story. Here's my classroom reality. From 1943 during the World War II days, when I was 5 years old at School 17 right across the street from my our house at 1600 Hutton Street, Troy New York, right up to the last class I took at The College of Saint Rose in Albany somewhere around 1995 and by then I was in my fifties, I lived a half century being groomed by some very good teachers. There were also a few just so so teachers whose names are lost to me. But then, and this is the fantastic part, I was gifted with some extraordinary teachers who just lit up my life and they remain in my storeroom of what I know and what I can still come to know. These teachers (mostly women although there were a few men) remain with me today and their lessons are still being taught and still being learned.

My scholarly inventory of 75 years has me ever sitting at a desk in a classroom. That's where I am at my most joyful, my most energized, most fulfilled. In a phrase -- most turned on. As a student I'm on fire, ready to go, ready to learn, ready to grow my mind, stimulate my brain, and reveal more secrets which very soon will be secret no more. I never once said "I hate school, or even "I'm so sick of school. For me there was never ever enough school. I still feel that way.

It started for me in kindergarten in 1943 with Miss Markham. There were no desks yet. On day one you arrived with a big bright ribbon from home which you tied to the back of a very small chair (I remember wooden, curved hoop back with spindles) and this is how you could identify your very own chair. I remember one day we made butter; each one of us got a turn at churning, like little Pilgrims. Then we brought crackers from home and this was our first classroom party.

After kindergarten at PS17, I went down several blocks (Janie holding my hand) to St. Paul the Apostles' for first and second grade in order to prepare for my First Communion. I don't remember sister's name but I do remember that we wore uniforms, and that once when sister lost her keys we all learned and repeated over again "Little Infant Jesus lost and found please help sister find her keys." The keys were found behind the piano. And I remember Father somebody coming into the classroom and sister quickly signaling us to stand respectfully and say in unison, "Good Morning, Father."

Then back to 17 for third grade. That was a dream year for me, right out of Hollywood. Our teacher, Miss Cahill, was movie star beautiful and she had a glittering diamond on her finger and she was engaged to a movie star handsome soldier (think Rita Hayworth and Clark Gable) who would pick her up dressed in his proper uniform, right in front of school in his Army jeep when he came home on leave. Later that year they married and Miss Cahill became Mrs. Schaefer. I loved everything I learned that year and in fourth grade with Miss Sweeney, including Palmer Method cursive writing, something which has never left me. Of course everything was about the war and in my third grade innocence I knew only of the patriotic and proud. I remember a photograph, now sadly lost, taken of me and a friend of mine, an African American boy classmate, and we're standing in front of school, smiling, dressed like twins; he in short pants, knee socks and striped polo-type shirt and I the same in a skirt. We are proudly holding a book of government saving stamps promoting the effort to help win the war.

Diversity was the best thing I came to know at School 17; children of every race and nationality. I remember one boy from Greece. His name is in my memory -- Constantine Quine – a name with such a musical ring to it. Other ethnicities were Native American, Hispanic, African American, Armenian, Italian, Polish, and of course English and Irish. This diversity was a real melting pot gift which I came to appreciate even more in later years when I was made aware of the evils of bigotry, racism, and hatred. At School 17, "stick with your own kind" was something that was never said to us, never occurred to us. All of us were *your own kind*, kids from Beman Park, from Troy New York, all patriotic American kids.

I finished 4th grade at 17 and then when the war ended we moved from Beman Park down the hill to 3 Eagle Street where my dad purchased our first home on the GI bill. This placed us in St. Peter's Parish. I started fifth grade and got used to being taught by the nuns. Sister Nicholas was a good teacher, smart and all that but she had little patience with misbehaving boys. I remember the whole class; row by row having to go up to her and one by one she whacked our palms with the ruler. As I recall, Sister meted out a harsher punishment to the boys (palms up palms down) who were to blame for us being disciplined since they had refused to turn in the guilty boy who had done the crime.

I have calm and pleasant memories of 6th grade. My teacher was a pretty young nun, something like Sister Edmund Catherine. That year I was home sick for several weeks with a scarlet fever type infection but not as serious; I think it was called scarletina. I was quarantined alone in my brothers' room in the dark and quiet. I remember Sister taking pity on me when I went back to school. One day I didn't have my homework which was unheard of for me. Sister saw I was getting anxious, ruffling through my papers and she spared me embarrassment and shame by not calling on me. When it was my turn. Nothing was ever said between us but I recognized her act of compassion.

The real terror came in seventh grade. Sister Hilda had the reputation rightly earned of being a real "battle ax." She took no guff from anyone but it was the boys who got the brunt of her temper. She called them names like "you bold stump" or "you lazy lump." She had the cleanliness/godliness thing down pat. There was a big, unkempt boy who smelled like he hadn't washed in days. Sister came in with a large cake of yellow soap (in those days that meant laundry soap i.e. Fels Naptha) and she sent him down to the boys room to wash, telling him he was big enough to be out working like a grown man not stinking up her classroom. But Sister was a good teacher. And there was a true heart hidden under that black and white habit. One example of her kindness, she would thank us for the little Christmas gifts we gave her and after the holiday vacation she thanked us again saying she had sent them – powder, handkerchiefs, note paper,-- to her "friends" serving time at Dannemora Prison.

Seventh grade was demanding and we did a lot of memorizing, taking at least one Regents subject – a course culminating with one of those scary tests the teachers hadn't made up, the official tests from Albany. She would walk up and down the aisles as we were taking the Regents exam. If she saw one of the boys in danger of failing starting to check off an incorrect multiple choice, she would silently elbow him until he changed his mind and made the correct choice.

And if I didn't have my milk money once in awhile she would call some boy up to her desk and say, "You've got a pocketful of money. Give me 8 cents for Little Spain's milk." (There were four of us sisters passing through St. Peters: Janie, me, Virginia and Marion so Little Spain was what she called me.) Sister also told me I better be as smart as my sister Jane who Sister said "was a pearl". She made sure all her seventh graders took dancing lessons over at the lyceum and saw that anyone who wanted a date for Easter was properly fixed up. There's much to thank Sister Hilda for.

In 8th grade, we were preparing to graduate and go to Catholic High. Our teacher was the principal, Mother Mary Alice, a gem.

She was the other side of the coin from Sister Hilda, calm, refined, maintaining quiet order with no shouting or elbowing.

Catholic High introduced me to another order of nuns; we had both Sisters of Mercy and the Sisters of Saint Joseph. Two of my favorites were Sister John Emanuel for Spanish, a CSJ, and Sister Dorothea, a Mercy, for English and Advanced English. Sister Dorothea loved my poetry. Sister John Lalande taught Secretarial Practice where I got to use for the first time the one and only electric typewriter. I left Catholic High a proficient future secretary. In addition to all the sisters, I also experienced our principal Father T. Gerald Mulqueen, who became a Monsignor in 1955, the year we graduated. Another great priest, Father Tom Phelan, taught mainly college prep students and I was a Business major so I remember having him only once in a 4th year Religion class and I was so impressed. He wore an English tweed jacket and he taught us a morality lesson about examining our conscience and understanding the meaning of false generalization.

Teachers lit up my life; broadened my life, opened doors in a learning castle I'm still exploring. They made me the student I always will be. Deo Gratias.

* * * * *

Week 20, April 18, 2013

Grandma Fisher Saves Me – Birds

I was waiting for Mom at a table at the Daily Grind on Third Street. She was late again this week, 5, 10, 20 minutes. I walked to the entrance, looked up and down the street, and tried her cell phone. "I was so worried," I gushed when she finally arrived.

My mother seemed annoyed. "Well, you did change our time, *twice*."

She was right. I have a very bad habit of thinking my time is more valuable than hers as I am working and she is retired. I checked myself on that one.

The food was delicious -- mixed bean soup, grilled chicken with fresh mango and red pepper slices on ciabatta, small side of tasty pasta, and triangles of fresh pineapple.

Mom took out her papers. She looked at me sternly. "You need to know, I have been in a *very bad place*. A frightening dark place. I was telling Dr. Van Dyne yesterday that I didn't know if I could go on. I wrote this in my journal...here, look." She opened up a notebook and read: "*You keep digging and digging and that leads to a burial. You're playing Russian roulette, a very dangerous game...*"

She stared at me. "Do you see? I was in a panic about how to save myself and, then, all of a sudden, as I was writing, there she was in my mind.... my Grandma Fisher.....and all of a sudden, my mood changed and I wrote this:

psm,4-14-13

Grandma Fisher Saves Me

You keep digging and digging and that leads to a burial. You're playing Russian roulette, a very dangerous game, and life is nothing if not a game of win or lose, life or death. Clutter is everywhere and I'm in a dark mood. Help is coming.

When we were kids, Grandma Fisher used to come and do necessary servile work at 3 Eagle Street. She dressed like a proud, refined, English matron, came in a taxi, tailored suit, wide-brim veiled hat, proper shoes that were almost elegant and tied; sturdy is the adjective that fits. She certainly had proper ladies gloves. But the exclamation point of her attire were the fox tails, draped over her shoulders. The neighbor kids sitting out on the porches at the corner of Ninth and Eagle Street knew someone pretty big deal had come to town when the Spain's grandmother arrived.

Grandma Fisher entered into our 3 Eagle Street world with a purpose: a visit to her daughter, our mother Evelyn, and to see us, her six grandchildren. She knew that two-story house and full basement would need a thorough spring cleaning, and her daughter would be overwhelmed. (And almost as an aside Grandma Fisher acknowledged her son-in-law, our father Charles. I remember hearing a respectful and never condescending, "Hello, Charles" and that was about it.) She left her prim, proper, neat, clean organized world over in Laconia New Hampshire where she lived with her only sister, our Aunt Cora, and she was most certainly on a mission and she most certainly had an agenda.

I want to put a calendar on the wall; April 1950 seems about right; making me about 12. I was the second oldest and well fit and able to help with the cleaning chores. Grandma Fisher was here to save us. She, the dark Protestant, proud, Eastern Star, English woman who was nonetheless a piece of the family fabric, a bolt of which was crammed wrinkled in a drawer in a butler's pantry at the very Catholic, mostly Irish 3 Eagle Street.

I'm still trying to save myself and this writing is about the cleaning lady who came to make us right. As Coleen and I in 2013 are working to write ourselves right, Grandma Fisher came to 3 Eagle Street to clean up our act – to 'Clean Us Right.' In this scene the proper lady has changed her wardrobe. She wears a clean housedress, work shoes, an ample white tea towel fastened back to cover all her golden hair. That's right, Grandma Fisher had beautiful; long golden hair which she wore in a bun. Family secret says she preserved her golden color by shampooing and rinsing using lemon juice.

I keep flashing back and forth between 1950 then and 2013 now. The now point is how do I save myself physically, emotionally, manage to get my act together. Peggy, do your laundry piled high in plastic bags, do your dishes, clean up your kitchen, bathroom, bedroom and somehow de-clutter papers, books, your round table covered with desk clutter: bills, notebooks, pens, tape, stapler, magnifier. The building people will be here this week to install new windows so be sure to take down the drapes, clear everything off the windowsills, move the desk away from the bedroom window corner.

Sometime in the next 48 hours finish your school days piece started last week and write something positive and creative for this week. Shower and shampoo somewhere in there.

Well back in 1950 Grandma Fisher was ready to work and we were never asked if we'd like to help. She enlisted us – we were her little army. This lady knew how to turn a neglected shameful mess into a clean shiny spotless work of art. I was one of that small army who dusted, polished, brushed, up the stairs, down the stairs, every spindle, nook and cranny, washed windows and mirrors. (A tin container of Glass Wax is etched in stone in my reverie.) We even learned how to polish silverware, can you imagine, I mean what was the point? My grandmother's second husband Harry J. Fisher (we called him Uncle Harry) owned a hotel which they both ran -- the Brownville Hotel in Brownville New York. We were taught by my mother and grandmother how to make a proper bed, set a proper table, what dishes made a proper table setting; (Proper was one of my grandmother's favorite words and we learned what was and what was not.) Literally we knew everything from soup to nuts and how many glasses and where they all went. Yes we knew about finger bowls. You'd have thought the queen mother was coming to dine at 3 Eagle Street.

To stay on point, I need to focus on how I will de-clutter my mind, my heart, my space, my place – a necessity if I am to save myself. What I want to do – no – what I will do is arm myself with all her cleaning aids, wrapped in the saving grace of Grandma Fisher. Her name was Grace Pearl, and it sounds like a prayer. In my Catholic classroom the nuns posted a reminder over the bulletin board that read *Cleanliness is next to Godliness.* But the real elbow grease scrubbing lessons about what made something clean I learned from my beloved Protestant, English grandmother who wore foxtails when she came to 3 Eagle Street.

Grandma Fisher, I honor you, thank you for all the lessons you taught me on how to get clean and stay clean. Your housecleaning lessons are still showing me not only how to de-clutter my life; but how to save myself.

⁂

"This is wonderful, Mom," I said. We talked some more and then I read:

cmp, 4-18-13

Birds

Just now running through Frear Park, joyful that I've been up writing since 4 am but stressed as I'm supposed to meet Mom in an hour and I still haven't thought of a "good topic" for the week, a robin landed in front of me on the path.

We made eye contact for a second.

In 4th grade, I wrote a poem about a robin. It won some contest and my teacher, Sr. Adrian Francis, asked me to read it in front of the class. As I did, one of the temporary caps on my front teeth (both broken in the shape of vampire fangs when I fainted face forward onto the concrete floor of the old St. Michael's church basement during a lst grade Brownie meeting) flew out of my mouth and landed on the desk of classmate Edward Gray, who promptly shouted, "Gross!"

Lying on the bottom bunk of my bed that night, still mortified, but resilient, I looked up at the silver zigzag frame of my sister Nor's bed above me and I thought about that robin poem. Yes, it was an awful day, but I was "a writer."

Anne Lamott explained the title of her iconic book on writing, *Bird by Bird*. As a child her brother was stressed out as he'd left a big assignment about birds until the very last night. "Just take it bird by bird, buddy," their father said, "bird by bird."

Last week, Anne spoke at Hudson Valley Community College here in Troy. My dear writer friend, Ellen Laird, a professor of English there, asked if I would autograph a copy of my picture book, BIG, to give to Anne's grandson, Jax.

"Of my gosh, Ellen, of course!" I tucked a "thank you" letter to Anne inside.

Always generous, Ellen arranged for me to have a front row seat. When Anne Lamott walked onto the stage, I cried, happy tears. Here was the person who had taught me more about writing than any other teacher, any other writer.

During the signing after, I showed Anne my well-worn copy of *Bird by Bird* – all of my notations, in different colored inks, over the past nearly twenty years. I told her I show young writers at schools those notations to teach how important it is to *catch our ideas on paper* as quickly as we can, "like fireflies on a summer night."

"I like that fireflies idea," Anne said, smiling.

A very gracious security guide obliged me and took two photos of us with my throw-away camera from Walgreens. I pray they come out.

Birds. I remember as a child giggling at the new ways my Uncle Mark who lived downstairs from us with Nana devised to keep squirrels from his birdfeeder. Crisco finally did the trick; those squirrels just kept on sliding. And how Nana had a pet bird she named "Billy Dick" (we're not sure why). She loved that little yellow bird and would occasionally open the cage so Billy could fly about her dining room.

One fall my mother stuck a suction-cup feeder to our kitchen window so we could see the birds up close. Nana complained about the seeds sailing down past her first floor kitchen window to the ground below. "They'll attract rats from the river," she said. Smile. Mom took the feeder down, then quietly put it back out there a few days later.

Birds. I recall the many happy times sitting in the cushioned window seat (my contribution to the design of the Guilderland house) with my young sons snuggled on my lap watching the birds that flocked to the large feeder I'd planted just outside the window. We had a colorful poster "Wild Birds of the Northeast" and we'd try and identify them.

Birds are in many of my novels. In the *Wedding Planner's Daughter*, Sam creates a garden labyrinth complete with bird feeders and baths. In the *Cupid Chronicles*, shortly after her Gramp dies, Willa sees a red cardinal and knows it's a sign of his love.

For me, this morning's robin was a sign to write free as a bird and the rest will follow and so I am less worried working on this book with my Mom and revisions of The Pink Sweater, not knowing if either will sell and God knows I need the money.

I trust the signs and keep on writing, bird by bird by bird.

* * *

As we were leaving the Daily Grind, I introduced Mom to my friend, Heather Lavine, owner of The Charles A. Lucas Confectionery, a hip new bar-restaurant on Second Street. Months ago when Mom and I were at a window table at The Illium Café, she looked across the street and read The Confectionery sign. "Charles Lucas? That was my father's grandfather's name. He owned a candy store."

"Really Mom? That bar was a candy store long ago. Do you think that's him?"

"Probably. I'll have to ask my cousin, Ned. He's the family historian."

Heather was happy to hear all of this. She said we must come see old photographs that she and her husband, and co-owner, Vic Christopher had discovered.

Mom and I made plans to have our next meeting at The Confectionery.

* * * * *

Week 21, April 25, 2013

Sweat – Okara Prayer

When I got to The Confectionery at 4pm, Mom was already happily ensconced in a booth chatting with Heather and Vic. It was nice to see Mom engaged like that. She looked so pretty dressed in royal blue and green.

"They have real napkins," Mom said, smiling, holding up a hand sewn cloth cocktail napkin. "Grandma Fisher is smiling down on these."

Heather poured us each a glass of water. Mom and I ordered two "small plates" to share – hummus and tapenade served with fresh crusty bread from The Placid Baker.

We read by candlelight. I went first:

cmp, 4-25-3

Sweat

I have been in such a wonderful zone this whole past week working on this third draft of the "pink book" -- going to bed early, setting my alarm for 4 am, cancelling and rescheduling to make more time for writing. Unfortunately part of my routine when I get in that "zone" is that I start eating more and more, especially toward the end of the story. Not so much with picture books -- I tend to work on these in short spurts and sparks -- but always with my fiction. A novel is like a pregnancy. It takes a long time.

I find that when I'm really in love....caring deeply about the characters... totally absorbed in needing to discover how will things turn out??!!.....I feel "fuller" each day.

As the months of writing pass, the book becomes bigger and bigger in me. I cannot separate myself from it. I'm waking, sleeping, dreaming book. All I want is to be with this book....just the two of us. Everything and everyone else is distraction.

Then all of a sudden it's "labor time" and I'm rushing to the finish and my emotions are crazy high and if I've done by job well I'm sobbing as I type that final scene.. .*the emotional weight of the story works*....and all while this is going on, quite frankly, I eat like a pig.

In "baby labor" they won't give you an ice chip.

In "book labor" I eat like Thanksgiving.

It is a glorious feeling to hold a finished manuscript in your hands --all those 150 pages or so have such a satisfying "heft" to them. *I made that! I did that!* But I would be mortified to list all the food I consumed before typing "the end" yesterday.

This morning, I stepped on the scales.

Holy #*#*#* !!!

I got off to clear that scary number, then stepped back on.

Holy #*#*#*!!!

(Coleen's note: Mom burst out laughing here. Yay.)

I slid the scale across the floor to a better spot.

Holy #*#*#*!!!

I gave the scale a few seconds to come to its senses.

Still no change. Stupid Scale.

Then I panicked because in just three days from now I have to be in a *fashion show*, a benefit for the YWCA's important "Women in Transition" program.

Columbus, my fashion show partner, will look awesome in his suit. He always does. After our "entrance" we're supposed to "mill around" and talk about the clothes we're modeling in case people wish to purchase them. The thought of all those people staring at my fat, fat, *fat* stomach put me into a cold sweat.

Sweat. That's exactly what I needed to do.

So I layered up and went for a run, one of my longest routes, and came home dripping. I may have only lost a few ounces, but I gained a good pound of better attitude.

* * *

"That's great, Col," Mom said.

"Thanks for laughing when you did," I said. Then Mom read:

psm, 4-25-13

Okara Prayer

"This offering today concerns one of the great loves of my life. And there's no way to be quick, concise or near complete so I'll just get to it. I have not yet figured out how to stop once I've started when I'm telling or praying or reading or writing or composing about my beloved Adirondack Mountains. Last night the pressure was on me again to choose something positive to share with Col and the something wasn't coming. So I opened my Nothing Book and started scanning through a lot of prose and poetry I've written over the years, and it soon came very clear to me that I could not go negative if I were to choose one of my Adirondack pieces.

I wrote this piece, *The Kingdom Ready*, on Saturday, August 26, 1995 (I was 57) as I took a meditative solitary morning walk over to Dureen's Pond at Okara Lakes. Okara is our childhood place and I was re-visiting a wooded place I knew as a child while renting a camp with my sisters. It took three handwritten pages when I copied it into my Nothing Book and I feel I need to apologize now if it seems to go on and on because of course it does go on a bit. Sitting in the Adirondack woods then and now brings me close to paradise and my words become prayer. Come back with me as I revisit paradise and I hope you can feel my awe and wonder."

(Mom stopped reading here. "Now..... picture me sitting on this decaying stump of an old tree...." then continued reading):

The Kingdom Ready

Here again. Thank God
These were our woods when we were young
Every smell, every sound, every taste
Every vision of God's giftedness.
A small rock, like a melon, just be-ing there,
Half in the ground, half above,
A white-gray swirl, still and stationery –
Just a rock on a bed of green.
Soft moss, plush and soft,
A cushion for my feet.
Just to look down on a morning walk –
To look down on grass, wild flower, twig and pine cone,
seventeen varieties of life in just the span of my arm
Trees that have kept house for me all these years
'You go and do what must be done

'I'll be here waiting for you
'We will keep the kingdom ready for your return.'
Every rock
Every pine cone
Every wild flower humble in its breathtaking beauty is here for me and waited.
As humans gone astray we prize the best seat in the house
But in what house?
The House of God in love with Nature is mine in my Adirondack kingdom.
My seat here - - a good, old tree now set to lie here on the soft ground
and nuzzle in, year upon year just to be permanent in timeless aging (how I go on)
about the best seat in the kingdom
Reserved for me this verdant and reflective morning in another August.
'Crystal clear' we like to say about so many unimportant nothings of our
ever racing minds—our rush to nowhere
In my kingdom the vision here of 'crystal clear' is the majestic fir tree –
intricate pyramid triangles pointing up to the heavens
and down into the mirror of the water.
God says, "The treasure is always pointing upward –
and reflecting downward in the same moment of time
The Inward/Outward of my dreaming,
My remembering,
My joy unbound
And my ceaseless crying of the cleansing tears.

May every child know the sweet and sacred rapture of a mountain wooded place –
of lakes and trees
Rocks and moss
Flowers, twigs and wild shrubs
Wedded all together in God's harmony
With symphonies of crickets, frogs and birds
The words and music of peace
in my Adirondack kingdom
All free
for you and me.
Amen

Week 22, May 2, 2013

Moving Through Loss – The Four Agreements

We met for dinner at The Red Front on Division Street, the place we'd order pizza from when I was a child. Sausage and peppers was our family favorite. Mom was waiting in a booth, wearing very springy purple and pink clothes and jewelry.

"You look so pretty, Mom."

"Thanks, Col."

I ordered a salad with balsamic vinaigrette and a fish dish.

"Oh, I need to order pizza," Mom said, "a small with sausage and peppers."

I smiled, secretly jealous, wishing I'd ordered that, too. I shared first:

cmp, 5-1-13

Moving Through Loss

With this book project with Mom, I've been moving through loss: my 28 year marriage, the family house my sons will forever call home, the Cape house they'll return to every summer, one day with their children, Popponesset Beach where I won't be building sandcastles with my grandbabies, "The Spit," where I won't be walking alone on windy winter days, soaking in inspiration, especially for the Willa books.

The tears come now and a mournful sob and I thank God for my writing.

Writing has always been the way I move through loss...writing in journals at 12, 13, 14, 15...in a home plagued by an alcoholic father whose short-cut method of parenting was to keep me in as much as possible.... no dating...no boyfriends, eavesdropping on his office extension to make sure I wasn't talking to a boy, spying in the window of the Red Front to check if I was really having pizza with *girlfriends only*.

From 8th grade on, I don't recall one substantive conversation with my father...us sitting at the table having a chat... no "so what's new?" or "how's school?" or "where do you want to go to college?" Actually, the one "real talk" I ever remember having with him was when new baby brother, Joseph Paul, died six hours after birth. Dad told me this *fascinating* story about how baby Joseph Paul was in Limbo and if we all prayed really hard enough we could get him moved up to Heaven. I was 8 years old.

That one central theme of "missing father" comes out repeatedly in my fiction... in *The Wedding Planner's Daughter*, *Sunny Holiday*, *Dreamsleeves*. Chatting with fellow author David Almond at a conference in LA once, I expressed concern that I might only have *one thing* to say in my writing!! David calmed my fears by sharing that for him, the loss of a beloved sister at a young age is that theme for him.

We writers write what we know.

Writing it right -- that's what Mom and I set out to do when we began this journey, agreeing to meet weekly for a year, to share pieces about what's good.

Nearly half-way to the finish line now, I ask myself, "how are you doing, Col?"

Well, I do believe I have finally "moved through" the loss of my father in my life. I have made great strides coping with the loss of my marriage and that Camelot golden dream. I no longer cry when I drop a son off at "his father's house" which was once my house, too, although last week when Dylan said they are refurbishing the trail I'd made behind the property which was let go wild after I left, I did get little teary, but now I think it's good. A trail is always a good thing; it invites one to walk and wonder. The loss of our family "Cape house" is still so painful when I think of how they gather there without me now; and I know I will feel ripped apart the day I sign off on the Cape house I impetuously purchased post-divorce, *chalk that up to really dreamy thinking*, because that will mean the end of my Cape Cod days. And poor Willa... how will she react?

All in all, though, what I've gained these past few years far outweighs the loss. There will be new grief to bear, certainly, that is the nature of being human, but I take comfort in knowing my writing will always be there, a silent, wise, and rock-solid friend.

⁂

"That's perfect, Col," Mom said. "Just perfect."

"What did my brother Joseph Paul die of?" I asked.

"Spina bifida. He was hydrocephalic," she said. "That was an unbelievably painful birth. His head was the size of a two year old." We talked more, then Mom read:

psm, 5-1-13

The Four Agreements

I'm a book person and that means I'm always reading a book – one at least and often two at the same time. As the addictive personality I am, I admit to being a compulsive over-reader. There's a pile of books on the floor next to my bed. In a small sampling, you'll find books on The Obamas, books from Dr. Andrew Weil, Dr. Wayne Dyer, Sister Joan

Chittister, the Dalai Lama; books on depression, books on spirituality. *A Course in Miracles*, I guess you'd call a tome, is well named -- it is a course that will take me the rest of my life to complete.

But the book I want to talk about now is a new treasure for me, *The Four Agreements* by don Miguel Ruiz. It came out in 1997 and was on the New York Times Best Seller list for seven months. I heard about the book when I saw Oprah interviewing Ruiz. She was remembering how she first heard of *The Four Agreements* when Ellen Degeneres asked her if she knew of it and then quickly added, "Oh, Oprah you must read it!" So Ellen praises *The Four Agreements*, Deepok Chopra calls it "a roadmap to enlightenment and freedom," and now in April Oprah (thanks again Oprah) brings him to me on a Soul Sunday morning. So I call the special book man in my life, Stanley at Market Block Books, and I order two copies – one for me and one for my grandson Ryan which I sent him with a love letter for his 19th birthday.

The book tells the story of the Toltec known for thousands of years in southern Mexico as women and men of knowledge and keepers of ancestral spiritual wisdom. Ruiz, who is a medical doctor, was encouraged by his grandfather, a respected Toltec spiritual master who said the time was right to pass on the wisdom to us in the present.

I'm moved and interested and enlightened about what I'm reading in The Four Agreements. Dr. Ruiz condenses all the baggage, dreams, judgments we have believed and lived by and reduces them to four agreements we make to ourself . He's offering a recipe for living our life, expending our emotional, mental and physical energy in a healing way. I agree when he says that love and forgiveness is the only way to heal. Our dysfunctional way of living is based on fear which creates anger, hate, sadness, envy and betrayal.

The four agreements are:

1) BE IMPECCABLE WITH YOUR WORD
2) DON'T TAKE ANYTHING PERSONALLY

3) DON'T MAKE ASSUMPTIONS

4) ALWAYS DO YOUR BEST

I'll be reading *The Four Agreements* regularly. I need to be reminded because I forget too often what is good for me and therefore good for the world. Dr. Ruiz knows and says the Toltec wisdom is aligned with all the great spiritual teachers including Jesus, Buddha, Mohammad, and Isaiah. In the final words of this small paperback he prays:

"Thank you, Creator of the Universe, for the gift of life you have given me. Thank you for giving me everything that I have ever truly needed. Thank you for the opportunity to experience this beautiful body and this wonderful mind. Thank you for living inside me with all your love, with your pure and boundless spirit, with your warm and radiant light.

Thank you for using my words, for using my eyes, for using my heart to share your love wherever I go. I love you just the way you are, and because I am your creation, I love myself just the way I am. Help me to keep the love and the peace in my heart and to make that love a new way of life, that I may live in love the rest of my life. Amen."

Week 23, May 10, 1013

My Mother Evelyn – The Power of One

Mom came to my house for tea. "I wrote about my mother," she said.

Even before she began to read, I felt choked with emotion. I never met my grandmother, never saw her face, never heard her voice. To know that she and I both walked this same earth for decades yet never talked or hugged or said "I love you"-- this woman who was my mother's mother -- is a great sorrow to me.

psm, 5-9-13

My Mother Evelyn

There are many mothers in our large family: me, daughters, daughters-in–law, (I call Kev's wife Colleen McNulty my daughter-in-love), aunts, sisters, nieces, and on it goes. But today I want to pay homage to and remember my own mother, Evelyn Florence Mary Cecelia Russell Spain Smith.

It dawned on me as I started this writing that this is the year my mother would turn 100 years old. She was born on December 21, 1913. As kids we always knew that her birthday was on the longest night and shortest day of the year – the winter solstice. I just don't remember if there were ever any celebrations for her; I hope there were.

When I consider my relationship with my mother I must first put aside the brokenness and experience the peace, comfort and solace in my heart. (The thing about being a writer is I'm immediately aware I'll never find the words.) Life is knowing the agony and life is knowing the ecstasy. I'm still learning that it's wrong to judge either my mother or myself. I know that in 1981 when I was 43 my mother and I hugged for the first time since we were separated when she left Troy when I was 15. This meeting was a miracle of the human spirit. For me, I never stopped carrying her in my heart.

My mother was kindness personified. There was that time she planned a special combined birthday celebration for me and my sister Janie as we turned 12 and 14. We had late January birthdays just 3 days apart and Mother said if we wanted to wait until February we could have a birthday/Valentine's Day celebration. The basement at 3 Eagle Street was put in very good order and decorated hearts galore as only my mother could. Our friends, boys and girls were invited. Mother prepared our favorite comfort foods, homemade goulash, Helmbold's little hot dogs and rolls. This was like no birthday we'd ever had or been to. There were records playing on the old Victrola; we sang, danced, played spin the bottle, pin the tail, and even played shuffle board on our real handmade stand up wooden treasure, a gift from our Aunt Marion and Uncle Bill in Cleveland Ohio.

I remember that my mother was always just very nice; never a harsh word. There was no bigotry in her, no racism, no looking down on anyone. One year when most of us were attending St. Peter's school she was elected president of the Mother's Club. I remember her being all dressed up and there is a picture of her with her sister officers. (My mother had suffered a terrible burn to her arm from wrist to elbow when the bathrobe she wore caught fire one Sunday at home when she was taking a roast out of the oven.) In her Mother's Club photo she wore long gloves which were fashionable and also hid the long ugly scar.

My story is entwined with my mother's story. I remember her love, a love that held me together over so many years when love seemed absent. So many fleeting fragments. I remember once as a young pregnant mother I was crying quietly as I tried to sleep. My husband Jerry asked me gently what was wrong and I said "I miss my mother." But there were never any words spoken beyond that.

As they say, we are all victims of other victims. So I don't judge – or at least I catch myself if I start. My purpose here is to remember that my mother gave me her love and she never stopped loving me. When I flew to Colorado for that joyful reunion after 25 years, my mother and I for three days in her senior apartment shared priceless heartspeak; that is a miracle in my life and so I could feel empathy when one of the things she said was "Peggy, if God was punishing me these 25 years, I'd gladly have 25 more." My mother had found someone who helped her mend her broken heart.

Mother's Day is letting me open my heart again to a woman who gave me life: Evelyn Florence Mary Cecelia Russell Spain Smith; born 12-21-13 – died 11-18-86. Beyond all the years of pain, longing and heartache her spirit is alive in me and continues to nourish my spirit. I've written about my mother over the years and I hope to share my prose and poetry with my children and grandchildren. Thank you,

Mother, for your gift of a mother's love. Help me pass it on over and over. Every day I am given should be a day of Mother's love.

⁂ ⁂ ⁂

"This is so beautiful, Mom," I said. "Thank you for writing this." Then I read:

cmp, 5-10-13

The Power of One

Running just now before 6 am, the only human on the trail around Frear Park, I thought of the topic I'd write about this week: the power of *one*.

Last Saturday I participated in the Hudson Children's Book Festival, a wonderful celebration of reading featuring nearly 100 children's book authors and illustrators from throughout the country, attended by some 5,000 children and their families.

I was scheduled to read my new picture book at 10:30 in the library. The festival was just beginning and no one showed up for my presentation. Not one person.

After a nice conversation with the librarian (I love librarians), I was packing up to leave when the door opened and in strutted a girl, aged 11 or 12 I'd say, with a woman I recognized as a teacher from a school I have visited over the years.

The girl approached me with this star-struck look, smiling, shaking her head.

"Ms. Paratore?" she said. "I am so, *so* honored to meet you." She thrust out her hand to shake mine. "Your book, *Dreamsleeves*, was the absolute best book I have ever read in my entire life. And trust me, I'm a reader. I just couldn't put it down. I lay on my bed reading for hours. My Mom said 'go to sleep,' but I just could not stop reading! I loved it *so much*. I got my language arts teacher to read it and now my class is reading it...."

I was so moved I began to cry, and then so did she, and her aunt (the teacher who brought her to meet me), and then the librarian, too.

This one girl's true affection for my work was worth more than any award I might ever win.

The power of one is a mighty power indeed.

⁂ ⁂ ⁂ ⁂ ⁂

Week 24, May 17, 2013

Sister Friends – Lilacs

We met at 3:00 at Mom's apartment. At her table by the window, she served our favorite Ginseng tea and a small plate of flower-shaped ginger cookies. As always, we laughed about the Dorothy Parker quote on the pink napkins: "I don't know much about being a millionaire, but I'll bet I'd be darling at it." Mom read first:

psm, 5-16-13

Sister Friends

"After the joy of Mother's Day I want to pay homage to so many women in my life. Springtime is here and looking out my fifth floor window fills my heart with sunshine, and blesses my eyes with unspeakable blue and white sky splendor and green trees like statues up to heaven. I have to be careful not to become pure melancholy; my want is to glean something of purpose and use from all this beauty, my goal being to make the world a better place.

So spring evokes the memory of a lifetime of women friends (I'll call them sister friends because sisters can be young, middle age, or growing old) who have walked with me through all my life as far back as I can remember. The thing about having a sister friend is so much more than having someone to hang out with or shop with. A sister friend is someone I have dreamed with, cried with, shared with, dared with, hoped with, a physical presence closer than arm's length who has helped me cope with life's challenges. I have been blessed with so many sister friends I could never name all of them. But my sincere hope is that every soul sister who has ever caressed my life knows that she has and knows how eternally grateful I am. A few names come to mind; countless memories remain.

Sally Brennan and I were next door neighbors up in Beman Park when I was just a little girl. My memory is that Sally and I would carry our dolls over to the big wooded lot (it's now the nurse's parking lot for Samaritan Hospital) and sit on the ground and play "poor". That's my memory, we played *poor*. Our mission was to protect our babies from any danger and make do with nothing but our own good sense and maternal instinct.

Many friends at St. Peter's School. In 7th and 8th grade classmate Nancy Lynch would sometimes invite me to have lunch with her at her aunt's upstairs flat just a few doors down from school. It was just the two of us; Nancy's aunt worked at Cluett Peabody's, the shirt factory on River Street. What a treat sharing what her aunt left for us to enjoy. Good food, great adventure, two friends sharing unconditional togetherness.

Phyllis Fobare and I played tennis when I was a freshman. She became a lifelong friend of my sister Virginia and Phyllis was there for me when I graduated from Catholic High and didn't have the traditional white gown (these were my motherless years). Phyllis lent me hers. Phyllis had the heart and soul of an artist and we connected deeply.

Decades and decades of women who were there for me. The memory can't grasp the names right now but the heart remembers. Sister Rita Shawn opened my heart to the needs of the homeless. It comes to me now that the women who were drawn to me and me to them are women who saw injustice and did something to correct it. What we shared was a need to heal a broken heart.

Today and for probably 20 years or more Mary Jane Smith and I share a sister closeness; so do Alice McLoughlin and Martha Walsh and Terry Page and Joann Coyle and the other women in our semimonthly discussion group. The rest of this writing could be nothing but name after name after name, decade after decade after decade.

Thank you, to all my sister friends. I hold you in my heart. You have walked with me, up close and personal. That means I am here today at age 75 because when I needed a love rescue, you rescued me. For every laugh, every smile, every tear, every banished fear, for validating my life in every way I can imagine, know we are eternally sister friends."

When it was my turn, I read:

cmp, 5-17-13

Lilacs

Jogging near my house just now, at several turns I was treated to the beautiful scent of lilacs. Lilacs in the month of May -- a wonderfully good thing.

I smell lilacs and I am a child in the dining room of that second-floor flat on High Street. My mom, sister Nor, brother Mike and I are gathered around the statue of Mary, rosary beads in our hands. There are candles and a vase of lilacs. There was a row of lilac bushes on our property and in May there were always bouquets. The year I married, at 21, and left, the lilac bushes had grown into towering purple trees of perfume.

Fast forward a decade and a half and I am at Hewitt's Garden Store in Guilderland purchasing lilac bushes to plant in my perennial garden. The following spring, purple blossoms bloomed and each year after that the trees grew fuller and more fragrant. There was always a bouquet of lilacs on our kitchen table in the month of May.

Fast forward another decade, and I am here in this house in Troy and there are no lilac bushes on my property. It's Mother's Day, a Sunday, the day my sons come back here from their Dad's. They brought a bouquet of lilacs from my garden.

They remembered how much I loved them.

Week 25, May 21, 2013

Irish Daisies – Ocean Mother

We met for tea at 3 at my house and, as my good topic today is dandelions, I served a Yogi herbal tea with Sarsaparilla root, cinnamon bark, licorice root, and "organic dandelion." Mom and I laughed about that. I read first:

cmp, 5-21-13

Irish Daisies

Recently I read that the English used to call dandelions, "Irish Daisies," probably meant in a disparaging way, something along the lines of those ignorant Irish foolishly thinking the yellow blooms were wildflowers instead of weeds.

Dandelions are *so not* weeds. Dandelions are delightful. I've loved them since my childhood. A dandelion is a powerful flower – there's a "lion" right in its name.

No matter the odds against them, dandelions find a way. They sprout out of cracks in city sidewalks, and parched abandoned lots. They survive no matter the poisons sprayed. You can't keep a dandelion down.

Today on my run I saw the full life cycle of dandelions: scrunched baby buds, squat yellow sons, tall slender divas with gold chapeaus, proud kings in crowns, white-haired wise sages, seed puff stars with full moon centers.

I stopped to pick a dandelion at each of these stages and carried them home in my pocket. I look at them now as I type these words.

Bro, the cat, came to investigate and now I have seed wisps all over my desk.

As I brushed them into the trash I couldn't help but believe that they will somehow find their way to soil and set down roots.

Dandelions persevere. Dandelions find a way.

Just like my Mom and me. Irish daisies.

⁂

"That's beautiful, Col," my mother said. "Just beautiful."

She took a sip of tea and shook her head and was silent for a long while.

"I'm really not doing well, at all," she said. "I couldn't write this week so I pulled a poem out of my Nothing Book." (blank book)

"That's fine, Mom. Your poetry is wonderful."

When she was ready, my mother read:

psm, 5-21-13

Ocean Mother

Thanks to Coleen I came to know Cape Cod in the nineties when she and Tony would invite me each summer. While the Adirondack Mountains are my soul's vacation dream, the Cape -- particularly the splendor of the ocean -- became a place where God's love was again revealed to me and I prayed my thank you in poetry.

On June 24, 1991 in early morning I took the short walk alone down to the beach, sat on the sand and took in the ocean at sunrise. Struck speechless, I had to pray my gratitude. After some opening words, I wrote two poems, Ocean Lover and Ocean Mother; today I will share Ocean Mother.

<u>Ocean Mother</u>

Ocean lady cleans her house
we take her offerings
leftovers
good enough for humans who rule the earth
Excuse me

Never ceasing her labors
love fest   no rest
Singing all the way
(If I stay I might sing with her)

She gently scrubs the rocks
This doesn't hurt
Sets breakfast down for sky avengers
Help a neighbor at your door

She opens her jewel box
pours out her birthing shells
The children cry to touch her face
I love you
now go beyond my arms

And all the while she sings a mother song
And sun pours warmth around her
You've worked so hard   so long

Her dignity arises
Ceases not her rhythm all the day
Her endless way of praying
working
singing

Creation bows
and takes her bounty
ever.

⁂ ⁂ ⁂

"Gorgeous, Mom," I said, reading over the poem again, savoring its beauty.

⁂ ⁂ ⁂ ⁂ ⁂

Week 26, May 28, 2013

Lost and Found – Happy Half-Birthday, Book

We met for dinner at Brown's on River Street, at first sitting at a table on the deck overlooking the river but, as it was threatening to rain, we moved inside to a table by the window. Mom read first:

psm, 5-28-13

Lost and Found

Today is my six month anniversary into an exercise in survival.

Six months ago I made a commitment to Coleen to write something positive once a week; and given that writing is my thing, my love, my hope, my prayer – what a simple and doable concept -- a once-a-week positive page or two. Really?

Well the demon called depression has kept right at me all these six months, telling me what I've heard a million times: forget it, it's no use, give it up, you're no writer, you're a fake, a fraud, and on and on.

Yet there's something about these 75 years that wants me to prove the negative demon wrong and the positive writing angel right. It's a simple concept; either you win or you lose; you grow the gift or you throw the gift away. Life remains a promise kept. Lost or found is a choice profound; and if I keep reading and writing the light will stay on. And I will find my life's purpose.

So I will pick up the pen and search on, and know that what I have lost I have found. And as I nurture my own heart, another heart threatened with losing itself may find itself -- in these words I'm writing. Happy six month anniversary.

"This is so powerful, Mom," I said. After a while, I read:

cmp, 5-28-13

"Happy Half-Birthday Book"

We are now 6 months into the writing of this book, a half-year forward from where we began on that snowy December day.

Blowing out the candles, I wonder: what have we accomplished?

Mom and I have kept our commitment to each other. We have showed up every week with something good we've written. Mom, even when nothing seems "good."

The writing has helped both of us and I do believe it will help others, too.

Going forward, I think we need to:

1. Write shorter pieces.
2. Edit what we've written to date until each piece is diamond bright.
3. Keep searching for a great title.

What say you, Mom: are you in it to win it?

* * *

Mom and I took a road trip to have lunch with my friend and super-talented editor, Nan Gatewood Satter. At a sunny table by the window at Miss Lucy's Kitchen in Saugerties, Nan generously gave us excellent advice, and much loving encouragement.

* * * * *

Week 27, June 9, 2013

The Bourne Bridge – Saving Mother Earth

Mom and I were both in such a bad places emotionally this week that we did not meet in person. We, did, however, write, so hooray for us. ☺

cmp, 6-9-13

The Bourne Bridge

This week has been hard. My Cape house still hasn't sold and the thought of those monthly $2,000 mortgage payments looming ahead with no end in sight wakes me up in a sweating panic at three am. And yet, I don't want my Cape days to end.

I went there this past week to write, sitting at the table looking out at the ever-changing parade of nature, swans gliding regally down the river, a proud mama duck with her gaggle of babies, like in the book *Make Way for Ducklings* my little sons loved.

While there I got an email from a feature writer at the *Times Union*. She was doing a story on Cape Cod and asked why I love it so. I told her what Willa says in the opening scene of *The Wedding Planner's Daughter*: "I love Cape Cod. I'll never forget the day we drove across that roller-coaster bridge, whitecaps sparkling on the waves below... Welcome home, Willa, welcome home." The Bourne Bridge holds iconic importance for me; it is a bridge back to memory and bridge forward to possibility. The ocean has been my greatest muse. The first drafts of all of my novels were written there.

Yesterday, after a movie, Connor and I went to lunch "my treat, Mom," at a new deli called Nosh on Western Avenue in Guilderland. The waitress recognized Connor. He had been in there last week with his brother, Dylan. Guilderland is their hometown.

My boys love me, indeed, and seem happy enough when they are with me here in the Troy house, but Troy will never have the heart-tug for them that it does for me. I am finally, five years later, fully realizing what a huge mistake I made in giving up both the family home and the family vacation home so easily. My attorney was furious, my therapist and friends all advised against it. I thought it would be the least painful route for our family. That Guilderland house was Tony's pride and joy. I could adapt elsewhere. It was always easier for me to deal with change.... to cross new bridges.

Well, at least it always used to be. I take solace in knowing that I loved the Cape for two decades before I ever "owned" a piece of it, something my wise son, Chris, reminded me of recently. I can always still visit Cape Cod. The Bourne Bridge remains.

* * *

psm, 6-9- 13

Saving Mother Earth

Who isn't having something to say about what's going on with our planet? Good old Mother Earth – either you're for saving her or you may as well just ignore her as in maybe she'll go away – as in she'll die of neglect. I'm interested in just about everything – my brain wakes up when some prophetic voice or some scholarly teaching voice, like maybe a NOVA program on PBS calls something of note to my attention, like I watched on PBS late last night all about the plight of Mother Earth: What's going on – who's keeping house – is there any point in taking any responsibility for destroying or saving her?

Most thinking people at least care; and even a chronic depression-challenged body like me knows that where there's life, there's hope. So we know we better clean house; germs and poisons and dried up water basins and melting ice glaciers and all that and more are contaminating Mother's cupboard, trashing her, doing their dirty work even though we prefer to look the other way. It's happening as we sleep.

Carbon monoxide gasses. Just one little thing to think about, reducing carbon emission. The experts say we are burning 9 billion tons of carbon dioxide a year. Is my carbon footprint soiling even spoiling Mother's clean floor? A yesterday reminder from childhood, "Don't forget to wipe your feet." Is it too late? Well maybe; but then again I hear Mother forgiving, "I'll give you one more chance." On our one planet Earth let's try to get along with our neighbors. (Note: Today China leads the world in the manufacture of solar panels. And also, China will build 400 nuclear reactors in the next decade. This isn't a contest to see who's right, who's wrong, who wins, who loses.) It's Mother's House and when some body loses, everybody loses. Let's make it a win-win game.

I'll try to clean up my act. It's not rocket science but is surely earth science. If in the past we have exploited our earth gifts – trees, whale oil, oil wells -- let's focus on sharing what's left and finding out what is reclaimable, sustainable, worth conserving and sharing. My recommended book this week is by environmental expert, science author and editor, Richard Alley, with a great title: *Earth: The Operator's Manual.*

Mother's not getting any younger.

She's waiting for her children to take care of her.

Week 28, June 14, 2013

Happy Father's Day – This Too Shall Pass

psm, 6-14-13

Happy Father's Day

Kevin Patrick, my youngest is over forty now -- oh how the years they go by -- and I've watched him for 14 years being a truly wonderful father, just the best father three lucky Irish kids, Liam, Lauren and Brendan could ever ask for. He and Colleen are A-list parents for sure. Kev's life is so worth celebrating – I feel it deeply because I've watched it happening – despite the fact that Kevin missed too much of the paternal love and guidance he needed and deserved growing up, due to his father's battle with alcohol. Kev has three older brothers who make great uncles but Kev is the only Dad among them and Kev's the one to whom I can say in love, Happy Father's Day, Kev.

Kev walked a very challenging journey and his teen years were full of obstacles that challenged, even threatened his survival and he has survived, turned his life to healthy goodness and has paid his dues. Kev has experienced the dark side, he has learned the better way and today he shows his children the better way. Thanks be to God my boy, now a man, is so many things: good husband, keenly intelligent, handsome, and healthy, a real gentleman, a great Irish wit and just an all around good friend and human being. He deserves every accolade and more. I'm his Mom, and I should know.

And there's more. Kev is celebrating big time this year because he has just accomplished a great academic achievement. The other day he called and left me a message and I'm so glad I kept the recording (mothers love to hear the sound of their children's voices). And here, before it disappears into cyberspace, here's the beautiful message Kevin left for me:

"Wednesday, May 29th, 7:04 pm. Hi Mom, it's Kevin. I hope you find this message well. I am calling to tell you that after five years of school and 9,700 hours of training I am officially a Journeyman Electrician. I finished today my final exams – totally finished -- and I'm certified. I love you and I just wanted to let you know that."

Kevin celebrates life and love and he works very hard at it. We all benefit from his gifts and I know he's only just begun. Congratulations, Son. Happy Father's Day.

cmp, 6-14-13

"This Too Shall Pass"

Last night I dreamt that I was lying on a city street, wedged between a tractor trailer and a car. I couldn't move. The trailer was backing up, soon I would be crushed. "Stop, help, stop!" I screamed, but no sound came out. I had no voice.

My writing is my voice. I am writing myself better right now.

I'm in a bad place emotionally but I know that *this too shall pass.*

Back in 4th grade, when my capped tooth flew out of my mouth and landed on classmate Edward Gray's desk as I read that robin poem, much to my excruciating embarrassment, I ran out into the hallway crying. I would never survive the shame.

My sweet teacher, Sr. Adrian Francis, in head to toe penguin gown, followed me out. She put her hand comfortingly on my shoulder and with kind eyes gently said, "This too shall pass."

I feel better just writing that: *This too shall pass.*

∗ ∗ ∗

Summer

Week 29, June 21, 2013

Muck and Muddle

cmp, 6-21-13

Dear Mom,

Today is the first day of summer, the half-way point of the year, the start of our third season of "writing it right." We began on a snowy December day, we wrote and met all through the winter and all through the spring. Now it is summer.

How are we doing, Mom? Are we writing ourselves "right?"

For many, summer is the happiest season -- sunny days, barbecues, vacations to enjoy. As I get older, summer has become my least favorite time of year. There is a heaviness to it, a feeling of stagnation, a muck and muddleness.

Here at the summer solstice point of our year-long journey, I feel we are in a muck and muddle place with our book. Yes, it is becoming very long and we will, of course, need to chop and cut when we begin editing, but there is something more.

Last week we were supposed to have lunch at the South Troy Diner. I waited and called. You said how sorry you were, but that you had really not been feeling well. Ordinarily, I would have called you to reschedule, but I found myself in such a mucky place too, worrying about whether it's right for Columbus to move in next month, scared about my finances, thinking about my three sons all together at the Guilderland house without me, and how next week they'd all be going to the Cape house where we shared so many years of happy family memories... I let myself slip under the mud.

I want to see where this journey leads us, Mom. We are creating something good.

But I worry... is our book becoming "wrong" for you, Mom? Is it moving you forward or causing you pain? Do you want to keep going? I hope so.

(Col's Note: Mom said she could not write this week.)

Week 30, June 27, 2013

Peg's Truth or Consequences – A Written Plan

We had a booth by the window at the South Troy Diner, a friendly comfortable place with good food and reasonable prices. Mom read first:

psm, 6-27-13

Peg's Truth or Consequences

I better start my healthy diet soon, my brain needs to be replenished with brain food – as opposed to junk food, fast food, bad food. Coleen and I are halfway through one year of our mother/daughter writing experiment and I've come to the conclusion that I want to continue with what I've started and bring it to a satisfying finish. Together we're figuring out how best to do that now and I feel as if I can get into it a little more and add to my share of this love task.

Continuing on means I need to stay healthy – or get healthy – in body, mind and spirit. One of my painful truths this week is I went to have my heart pacer (defibrillator) checked. Not a bad report, could be better, and Mary Ellen the technician (a physician's assistant) monitored how my heart was behaving and gave me a pretty good report. She said the battery tested strong; that there was still a speeded up heartbeat which was something they would continue to monitor. It had happened 11 times since my last checkup 3 months ago, but was not a major concern because each time this arrhythmia occurred it lasted only a few seconds and then returned to a normal beat. It's something they will continue to monitor. Nothing of concern on my EKG. My blood pressure was up a little which did not surprise me.

The real painful truth was when I stepped on the scales and saw how much weight I'd gained since my last visit. I was looking at a number that made me nearly 50 lbs. overweight. That's the real stressor, physically, and of course this equates to real stress emotionally.

None of this is new information but I do feel a new determination to do something about the bad shape I'm in. Taking care of me is all about facing the truth. It's simple – I can either follow the truth, or deal with the consequences.

And to tell the truth as I write this, there's definitely something positive in my thinking today. I met with my psychotherapist yesterday -- I've been seeing him every other week. As I was leaving after our visit I shared with him that I feel a positive energy when I talk with him. I've never said anything like that before. And I also want to say to my daughter Coleen if I haven't said it before, thank you for your gentle persistence, for urging me to give this project a try. It feels like I'm going in the right direction and feels like we're half way home.

* * *

"Oh, Mom," I said. "That's wonderful. I'm so happy for you."

cmp 6-28-13

A Written Plan

Writing it right...writing it right...how can I write myself right today?

I am in such a state of turmoil, physically sick to my stomach. For the past several weeks now, I have been agonizing over whether Columbus should move in. I met my ex, Tony, for a drink that turned into dinner as we had so much to talk about, five hours' worth, so much shared history. After, I wondered, is there still a possible future with Tony?

I told Columbus I wasn't ready for him to move in. He accepted that with great dignity and kindness. We agreed to keep things as they are, dating exclusively, but not living together. I love Columbus, and yet, I worry something is missing. We say "I love you" countless times each day, but sometimes have little to talk about.

Three days ago I broke up with Columbus, only to feel such tremendous pain that I drove to his place to say I'd made a mistake. We reconciled, only to have doubts fester up inside me all over again the next day. Tony and I met for coffee.

I love the life Tony and I built together, but am I "in love" with him? I am "in love" with Columbus, but can we build a real future going forward?

Yesterday I had a long conversation with a wise friend (FM) who helped me gain clarity that this isn't a Columbus vs. Tony thing. What is really eating me up is concerns about my career and future financial security, and what's my next work in the world.

Late yesterday, I broke up with Columbus again. He packed his things and left with a surprising lack of anger, perhaps the result of twenty years in the military and that built in self-control, discipline and strength. I sobbed, then felt relief, then woke up at midnight in a panic missing him, tossing and watching the clock, 1, 2, 3. This morning I texted him: "I said we have nothing to talk about and yet our first and last words to each other every single day are 'I love you.' Maybe that's all that really needs to be said."

Columbus was so kind. "One day at a time, Luv."

Just now Tony emailed to ask about dinner tonight. How do I feel about that? What do I want? I don't know. What do I need? Resolution.

In the midst of this, I wonder, am I pushing away love? Maybe I am so close to true happiness that my protective shield has gone into overdrive. Please God, don't let that shield imprison me in loneliness. I want to share this one brief beautiful life with another. I pray for discernment and resolution.

After writing this I went for a Zumba class, then ran 3 miles. While I was running God gave me an answer. *Make a written plan.* When I got home I did:

1. Lose 5 pounds.
2. Get my hair styled and buy some new clothes.
3. Set new writing goals.
4. Find funding for Read-Write-Roar-Return.
5. Stay completely away from both Tony and Columbus for a full week – no calls or texts and see how that feels.

After writing this, I felt so much better.

* * *

"I think your plan sounds great," Mom said.

* * * * *

Week 31, July 3, 2013

Blessings of Freedom – Labor

Mom was waiting for me in a booth by the window at Manory's. Our delicious sandwiches were served with slices of fresh ripe red watermelon, *yum*. Mom read first:

psm, 7-3-13

Blessings of Freedom

My feelings are all over the place but let me settle down on one truth: I am a free citizen living in a free country. Freedom to think, feel, speak, write – in other words, to champion freedom. All of that freedom is almost more than I can wrap my head around. So let me remember on this day of liberty and freedom for all, the countless of my brothers and sisters for whom freedom and the blessings of liberty do not exist.

The blessings of freedom – those words – remind me of a loving God who has breathed life and liberty into every soul. How is it that I was one of those souls spared the evil reality of discrimination, racism, hunger for power, hatred in all its manifestations? I've never been incarcerated for my beliefs, never been tortured, never been refused the right to vote. I remember writing letters with Amnesty International on behalf of prisoners of conscience who were being tortured and imprisoned simply for what they believed. Right here in my hometown I remember tutoring a young black man who wanted to be a firefighter because it was a right that was supposed to be made available to him and the truth was - there were very few black men serving in those ranks.

If I pray for America what am I praying for? A perfect place of freedom for all? Of course not. I can't do or be anything without recognizing the gift that I am. I must breathe freedom, and speak and act to benefit those for whom freedom is just a dream or worse yet a never to be fulfilled reality.

I try not to get all red white and blue in superficiality here in my hometown, the birthplace of Uncle Sam. I express thanks, as in I can't thank you enough, to a loving God for the freedom I've been given and a hope that I can share and speak for those still waiting for the liberty and justice meant for all. In my morning prayers today I came upon these words of Marianne Williamson; and her prayers are my prayers.

"Dear God, We join in prayer to celebrate this nation and surrender its destiny to You. ...We ask that God's spirit now fill our hearts with righteousness. ...May we play our parts in the healing and the furtherance of our country....May we be cleansed of all destructive thoughts....May judgment of others, bigotry, racism and intolerance be washed clean from our hearts....May our minds be filled with the thoughts of God...May this nation be forgiven its transgressions...May our lives be turned into instruments of resurrection, that the sins of our fathers might be reversed through us...May this country once again become a light unto the nations of hope and goodness and peace and freedom....May violence and darkness be cast out of our midst...May we be renewed....

Dear God, please bless America. Amen."

* * *

Seeing how much we had enjoyed the watermelon, our friendly waiter brought more, "compliments of the house." And then I read:

cmp, 7-3-13

Labor

I wish I could report "bright and sunny with a chance of happy," but this has been another week of muck and muddle, worry, confusion, *angst* in both my personal and professional life. I feel lost in limbo. I just want this to be over. Now.

Thank God for my dear friend, Pauline Kamen Miller, who sends gentle text messages "checking in" and suggestions we "meet for tea" as I've become so isolated.

Last night I went to bed at 6, pulling the covers over my head, hoping for some peace. I slept for three hours, then tossed and turned all night.... *please, God, help me.*

This morning I had such a pit in my stomach. It's as if I'm carrying a 50lb iron weight around in my gut. The moment I sat in my blue chair to pray and set my intentions for the day, I began sobbing....deep mournful wailing like there had been a death. I said my gratitudes and asked for discernment and serenity.

Then, minutes later out running, I recalled Mom sharing how when she was twenty and pregnant with me, no one told her how horribly painful labor would be, but after what a miracle it was to hold me. I thought of my own long, painful labors and then the profound joy of holding my babies, first Christopher, then Connor, then Dylan.

Perhaps I am in a metaphorical state of labor...heavy with the weight of something new that has been gestating inside....feeling the early contractions, the nausea, the lethargy and sleeplessness, the worries.... will this baby be okay?

Labor hurts, yet without it, there would be no birth. I cannot control it. Labor leads the way. Today I trust it will be to something good. And as I recall from my baby labors, until it's time for that final push, the only thing I can really do is *breathe*.

Week 32, July 11, 2013

Good Bye, Depression – Man of My Dreams

We met for lunch at Bruegger's on Congress Street by Russell Sage. I read first:

cmp, 7-11-13

Good Bye, Depression

Two weeks ago, Mom, you said you had decided to continue on with our book project, but then sadly added: "I hope I live long enough to finish it."

You will, Mom. **You will.** I won't settle for anything less.

Then, after our book is published and we finish our wild schedule of publicity tours and publication parties, I will help you embark on your next adventure.

Your memoir, perhaps?

Life is not done with you yet, Mom. You still have so much wisdom to share, light to shine, gifts to offer hungry hearts.

Remember those ugly orange life jackets you made us wear as kids when we went out on a boat at camp on Burden Lake? Well, last November, when the depression in you was bleaker than I'd ever seen it, and I was terrified of losing you, I imagined this book as a life jacket around *you* as you floundered on the stormy sea with a sturdy rope so I could pull you safely back to shore with me week after week. I hoped if you made a commitment to me (you always keep your promises) and wrote (you are always happiest when writing) that this project would keep you afloat until the depression subsided.

I have learned from you that depression is a monstrous guest who shows up without warning, stays as long as it damn well pleases, makes you miserable for what seems like an eternity and then, poof, it's gone again. You don't know when it will, but *it does go away*.

The depression monster has clearly overstayed its visit this time, Mom, but it is leaving. I see such encouraging signs in you. The dark clouds are dispersing; there's new light around you. You are *you* again. Happy New Day, Mom.

So good bye, depression and don't come back. Let the door whack you where the Good Lord cracked you. Let the knob hit you where the dog should have bit you.

(old Southern sayings compliments of Columbus ☺)

* * *

Mom burst out laughing here. "I hope you're right about the depression."

She spoke with mild, but genuine excitement about a new healthy eating plan she's begun, talking about the types of food recommended. And, then, I must admit, my mother absolutely amazed me with what she'd brought to share:

psm, 7-10-13

Man of My Dreams

Is there ever a day that isn't a day of the heart? I don't think so. This woman's heart is a many splendored thing and I'm only 75 as the calendar counts my love story. And is there ever a time when you can't be *young* at heart -- you know, when fairy tales can come true and it can happen to you? I think there is – in fact I know there is. This is my dream come true I kid you not. I get all romantic if I see a good love story and that's what happened for me this week. And this story is all mine, well, his and mine. I imagined him, I dreamed him, and I made him mine and I want to tell someone so thank you for being that someone. I'm talking about the man of my dreams come true. He's adorable and I know he's the right one because I know how my heart feels (a woman just knows) and this dream come true of mine speaks to me; tells me that I am the dream that came true for him. Now because we are together, our lives are forever changed and we've only just begun.

His name is Devon Casey O'Rourke. He's from Ireland (you think?) from County Wicklow where we've spent time together and will go back soon. This Irish boy is a man of course, about three years my senior and that's the last time I'll use the word senior in this love story.

Devon stands tall; just under 6 feet. That's nice when we walk down country lanes together which is often and I pause to take a minute's breath and I rest my head over his heart; that's a perfect fit. It's his smile that starts me singing – when those two dimples come out of hiding and those heaven-blue eyes and long eyelashes send promises that he wants always to be here for me and protect me. I love to run my fingers through his full head of wavy hair which isn't black, brown, or blonde, but almost rusty.

Devon is everything I ever wanted the man of my dreams to be. He's, strong, kind, intelligent, a gentleman in every way. He has a delightful, playful sense of humor that in the blink of an eye can turn serious and sincere when there's something to be serious and sincere about. We share the same Catholic faith and we go on and on sometimes about how our faith has disappointed us and how we are hopeful things can change. We're old fashioned sometimes and do go on about the good old days, but at the same time we champion the changes we want to see. We're that way when we talk faith, politics, family, old friends, new friends. Life is exciting and full of promise but we're careful to take time to enjoy just today, because today is the best gift ever.

Devon loves that I love poetry; he reads to me and wants me to read my poetry to him. We sing and dance together, and party whenever two or more are gathered.

If you were to ask me to sum up what Devon is for me I'd have to say he's the best of everything I have loved and admired in every man woman or child in my life's experience. We plan on taking care of each other all the way down this awesome road of life and love.

So yes, of course it's possible to dream, it's a requirement of faith. I dreamed my dream and it came true and I wanted to share it with you. And because I often find my words in a song my medley includes love is a many splendored thing -- and fairy tales can come true it can happen to you -- and not to go on and on let me close by saying Dear Devon, just thought I'd drop a line, see you soon, and P.S. I love you.

* * *

"Wow, Mom. This is great. Good for you! I'm so happy to hear this. You still have time, Mom. You will find him. You just have to put that intention out in the world. And now... you have."

* * * * *

Week 33

(We were both in dark places and did not write or meet ☹.)

* * * * *

Week 34, July 22, 2013

Plea for Peace – My Bucket List

We met at Mom's apartment for iced tea. We both shared about still being in bad places, each giving the other as much support as we could muster – my mother always doing a *much better* job at that than me.

"You don't get to live life without pain, Col," she said. "That's how we know to appreciate the joy." And then she read:

psm, 7-22-13

Plea for Peace

I'm praying for peace and praying for the courage to make a difference. I'm so distraught over the still surviving racism we are living and breathing this very moment right here and now. The young man Travon Martin in Florida who won't get to live his life, fulfill his dreams, shot dead -- point blank. And how easily too many of us determined well in a way he asked for it. Yes, we were broken hearted for his mother, felt her despair, did not in any way justify the neighborhood watchman who pursued the boy, watched all the replays of what happened, why it happened, and how the shooter was found not guilty.

I think of my own city of Troy and I know there are young black men right here and now who have already learned the only way to survive is to carry a loaded gun that can kill someone before someone kills you. I think of our children who breathe a destiny of desperation. We have neighborhoods of poverty where it is considered unsafe to walk alone, never after dark. It feels an almost useless endeavor to end the racism that is sickening the American spirit, sickening my city.

We are endowed by our creator with those inalienable rights: life, liberty and the pursuit of happiness. We have destroyed that pursuit for hundreds of years because we labeled our brothers and sisters unworthy -- Native Americans, slaves, women, our gay and lesbian brethren even those whose freedom of religion didn't fit what someone thought was the one true religion. The ghosts of our sins cry out to us: Please – enough.

If a teenage boy walks home and never arrives, dead before his time, it is because someone forgot to honor a human life. We are all asked to reach out and respectfully invite a conversation – a conversation of reconciliation. Can we make our young black citizens feel safe – and yes the word is safe – safe enough so they are able to express their disappointments, insecurities and loss of hope? We are way overdue for a let's sit down and talk time. President Obama knows what it is to have experienced racism; so does sadly every young black man here with us today.

My plea for peace begins with me. Evil will continue to survive, to kill the dreams, the hopes, the very lives of our young people until we confront that which is destroying us.

Let's begin a conversation of reconciliation.

⁂

I am always amazed at how my mother, despite the agonies of her own situation, always keeps up on the major issues of our day and always cares more about the suffering of others. She is truly the most Jesus-like person I've ever known. In so many words I told her that and then I read:

cmp, 7-22-13

My Bucket List

1. Write a New York Times best-selling book.
2. Write more Willa books. (I pray for a contract soon!)
3. See my three sons in happy relationships, doing work that brings them joy.
4. Read to my grandchildren the same books I read to their fathers.
5. Be happy with a partner for life.
6. Finish this book with my Mom, get it published, and meet Oprah.
7. Visit Ireland again.
8. Continue to make a living from writing and teaching.
9. Do something special for the girls of Troy.
10. Have a place by the water again.

⁂

"I like that list, Col," my mother said.

"Thanks, Mom. I'd love to hear yours."

She laughed. "Are you kidding? I'm just lucky I'm alive."

* * * * *

Week 35, July 30, 2013

Road Trips – No More Cursive

We met for lunch at Spill'n the Beans. I read first:

cmp, 7-30-13

Road Trips

When my three boys were little, I took them on "adventures" – to the library, playgrounds, museums, shows at Steamer 10 in Albany, on nature hikes at Five Rivers, picnics at Indian Ladder Farms, swimming at Tawasentha Park…

As they grew older, their schedules filled with school, sports and friends. Life was planned out, structured, marked on the calendar with scant room for spontaneity.

Then, one summer on Cape Cod, I got this notion to do a "road trip."

"We'll just get in the car tomorrow morning," I suggested, "and we'll drive in a random direction and when anyone sees anything that looks interesting, we'll stop."

The boys thought this sounded great. We were up and on the road early.

The day began with bagels, then miniature golf, then bowling at an arcade, then lunch, ice cream, a movie, finally dinner, where Connor ordered lobster for the first time. I took pictures at every stop, secured now in a little album called "our first road trip."

More than a decade has passed since that first road trip, but the concept is firmly rooted in our family. My preference is for a road trip with just one son at a time as it is such a joy to be able to focus on that one child, fully present, eyes to eyes, heart to heart.

I will never forget landing in Las Vegas with Chris as we celebrated his 18th birthday, lights rising up out of the desert night; or standing at the abyss of the Grand Canyon with Dylan, breathing in that crystal clean air, soaking in the wonder. Just last week, at his suggestion, 20-year old Connor and I "road tripped" to Washington, D.C...toured the Capital, the White House, the Martin Luther King Memorial. He chose restaurants from his I-phone... no lobster, but lots of laughs and fabulous memories.

Who knows when the next road trip will be or with which son....that's the beauty of the concept....the random, unplanned, *surprise* of it all.

A road trip is a very good thing.

psm, 7-30-13

No More Cursive

Things are changing. Well, of course things are changing; it's the 21st century. Something named Information Technology – IT for short--that whole body of knowledge explaining how computers work, how they have changed, improved, modernized, revolutionized the way we talk to each other. IT has been for at least fifty years now something you study like English, Spanish, nursing, law, auto mechanics, or anything else you'd like to become proficient in. (Oops, think I ended that last sentence with a dangling or hanging participle; but on second thought that's probably nothing to get hung up on anymore.)

I was a bright business student back in the fifties back in Catholic High when I was a teenager and knew I would earn my living in the business world. Typing, Shorthand, Bookkeeping, Office Practice all that became part of what I had to learn and did learn. Still today my fingers can fly over the keyboard or with pencil in hand I can scroll the Gettysburg address using the same Gregg Simplified learned sixty years ago.

But I have to admit I have kept up only very little with the new technology. What's second nature to my grandchildren -- Facebook, Twitter -- is not second nature to me. Of course I can sit down at a keyboard: the a-s-d-f-j-k-l-; is still where it always was on the keyboard (thank God but I can't be certain that won't change) and so far it remains in place just like you still count one to 10 – 1- 2- 3- 4- 5. As for texting, I'm not even a beginner. As a business student in the fifties I became proficient at whatever I studied, for example, the manual typewriter. And long around 1953 I was introduced to something new and better, a term -- three capital letters – IBM – then the best there was and grooming itself to become king of the computer world. I embraced that new knowledge and followed it.

But now I have to sit with the hurting truth that cursive writing is no longer deemed important. You mean soon it won't BE anymore? Oh how can they do that? It's how I write. I have years of books and journals pouring out my life, telling my story. It's how I talk to my children, grandchildren, siblings, friends - when I send a card or write a note or a letter one page or pages long.

Will my heirs even be able to decipher what I said?

If they want to describe their grandmother as old fashioned they could just say she still writes in cursive. I guess it's not so much that I spent months even years perfecting what we call Palmer Method. It's that my penmanship identified me as me. What I wrote is what I said. That's me talking. The dictionary defines cursive as merely the joining together of letters to make words, but it's how I was able to tell my story, what I had to learn in school, as normal as learning to ride a bike or roller-skate.

Let's sum this up. I choose never to stop writing in cursive. That's not rebellion – that's just who I am. Who says I have to unlearn my handwriting. To even attempt that would mean I'd have to stop writing, never pick up the pen and tell a story. Pen in my hand opens the door from my heart to my heart's intentions. Not to have that would silence me and no one is asking that of me. I have more to say before I finish my last chapter. And I'm still close to the keyboard, yes; but my cursive handwriting, well that's who I am, what I am.

⁂ ⁂ ⁂ ⁂ ⁂

Week 36

(Col was away teaching at the Cape Cod Writer's Center.)

⁂ ⁂ ⁂ ⁂ ⁂

Week 37-38

(Peg had a heart attack—in ICU, then progressive care.)

⁂ ⁂ ⁂ ⁂ ⁂

Week 39, August 28, 2013

A Little Setback – Magic or Miracle

The fact that my Mom entitled her piece this week "A Little Setback," is a mind-boggling testament to her amazing strength and courage. If her pacemaker had not kicked in a few weeks ago, she would most likely be dead. I will let her tell the story.

We met at Francesca's restaurant on the corner of 5th and Broadway. There was a bustling lunchtime crowd. The chef-owner, Francesca, and colleagues Annalisa and Antionette treated us like family. Our sandwiches were delicious.

When I whispered to my mother that there were some handsome men her age (I could tell by their banter they were lawyers) at the table next to us, she checked them out, smiled at me and said, "I'm still waiting for Devon Casey O'Rourke."

"Well maybe he materialized," I said and we laughed out loud.

I actually entertained the thought of approaching one of the men (definitely Irish) to introduce him to my Mom, but in light of her recent heart attack, I exercised restraint.

As we ate, Mom pointed to a framed issue of the *Troy Record* newspaper on the wall, an ad for Frear's department store, from a time when "house dresses" cost $1.29.

"Your Aunt Virginia did the art for these ads and modeled for the store as well."

Mom read first:

psm, 8-28-13

A Little Setback

I'm back in front of my computer (I almost said typewriter), so things should be back to normal but not quite. A big big happening happened to me earlier this month on Tuesday, August 13th. As sisters do their sister thing it was a big Janie day as Janie was scheduled to enter Samaritan Hospital for knee surgery and Mim and I were going to pick her up and be with her. It was raining, 9:30 a.m., and I was inside the entranceway waiting for Mim when without warning I felt this explosion-like thing go off inside my chest. For a second I looked up to see if something had crashed through the ceiling but then quickly realized: Oh my God this just happened inside me.

Along side helping Janie (this was after all her day) with Mim and other helping people I was able to reach Dr. Atalay's (my regular heart guy) office who it turns out was not on duty but Mary Ellen King, cardiac nurse practitioner who has checked my defibrillator several times on a regular basis said she would examine me at 1 pm. This time the test showed I'd had rapid heartbeat a lot of times in recent weeks and that's why the defibrillator went off (my big shock). What it was doing was shocking my heart back into a regular heartbeat. She then said things had gone back to normal but she just wanted me to have an echocardiogram before I left. Well it turns out the echo showed not a heart beating regularly but a heart beating dangerously fast and *no I could not go home* – I was transported immediately next door to the Samaritan Hospital. After two days in intensive care I was able to be transferred to coronary care and later that week I was discharged under the care of the new heart man in my life, Dr. Morris.

So now it's August 28, 2013 and I'm healing. My daughter-in-law good nurse practitioner midwife Colleen McNulty has shared her nursing skills, even writing me an easier to understand list of daily meds (I take 9 meds every morning and 6 every evening.) Colleen kids me and says "I think you were a cat in another life – you have lived at least nine lives." I'm up to my ears in taking meds, weighing myself to watch for swelling or unusual gain or loss, cardiac low salt diet, trying to walk 10 minutes every day. I've called my Cardiac Care Team (three times just this past weekend when the office is closed and you get whoever's on call. But all my care has been superlative – prompt, intelligent, caring. I keep pinching myself to say Hey Peg you're not dead yet (Yes this was yet another close call.) – so keep on keeping on.

Yesterday's snail mail brought me a card from a longtime church friend Marge Carroll who wrote me (in cursive, thanks Marge.) It sums up what so many of my kindred souls, family and friends have said and done for me:

> "Hi Peg, I haven't seen you in awhile and heard you had a little set back. I want you to know you're in my thoughts and prayers. If there is anything I can do for you, please call. Love and best wishes, Marge."

I'm alive at 75 and today on the 50th anniversary of The March on Washington and Martin Luther King's passionate ever enduring words of truth, courage and hope, I am re-invigorated, reborn, revitalized and committed to healing Peggy with the help of my caring love team. A little setback turns out to be a new lease on life.

⁂

"Hooray!" I said. "This is wonderful, Mom. You sound so positive."

"I am," she said.

"It's like the depression doesn't matter anymore," I said. "Thank goodness for heart attacks, huh? And you won't believe this, but I wrote about Margie Carroll, too."

Then I read:

cmp, 8-28-13

Magic or Miracle

Magic or miracle, superstition or saint's petition, by whatever name, when we need a wish granted, perhaps if we can suspend logic for just a bit, we can still step through the veil to that innocent, wonder-filled realm where anything is possible. I visited that world often as a child. A chance encounter in the market last Sunday made me think life might would be so much easier and fun, too, if I could allow myself to *believe* like that again.

Margie Carroll, a long-time friend of the family, was at the deli counter in Price Chopper. We chatted about relatives. Margie said her daughter, Krista, just sold her home on Cape Cod. I shared how stressed I was that my Cape house wasn't selling.

"Did you put St. Joseph in the ground?" Margie asked.

"What?" I was immediately intrigued.

"Don't you know?" Margie said. "St. Joseph is the patron saint of houses. If you put a statue of St. Joseph in the ground and pray to him, he'll help you."

I burst out laughing (in a nice way).

"No, seriously," Margie said, smiling. "It works. Trust me. You can buy a little statue at O'Connor's in Latham. It may even come with instructions."

"Instructions?"

"Well, you don't really need them," Margie said. "Just put him in the ground. Head first or feet first. It doesn't matter which."

"Thanks so much," I hugged her, feeling greatly encouraged. "I'll try it."

I haven't put Joe in the ground yet, but the notion of it.... *the idea of it*.... has brought me much joy. I'm going shopping today.

I think I'll plant him sideways.

⁂ ⁂ ⁂

"Oh that's great," Mom said. "I'll have to write Marge a note."

Leaving Francesca's, I once again resisted the urge to connect my Mom with one of those nice Irish lawyers.

⁂ ⁂ ⁂ ⁂ ⁂

Week 40, September 3, 2013

Extreme Dreams – Unexpected Invitations

We met at B-rad's Bistro on 5th Avenue. It has a hip NYC bistro vibe and the food is awesome. Talented chef/owner, Brad Stevens, is a neighbor of mine. We ordered the Grilled Portabella Mushroom, Fresh Spinach and Red Peppers sandwich and the Chicken Teriyaki Wrap with Cucumber Wasabi Slaw. *Yum*! Mom read first.

psm,9-3-13

Extreme Dreams

Her name is Diana Nyad. She's the latest in my list of remarkable women who have come into my life to teach me. This weekend I watched Diana (pretty much me and my TV) as she completed her 35 year old dream – she swam 110 miles non-stop from Cuba to Key West Florida. Diana Nyad accomplished this feat, described as beyond remarkable, at 64 years of age. This lady followed her dream and lived her life never letting her dream vanish.

Me – I'm working at my dream which is to stay alive long enough to complete my gifts of writing and speaking out. That's what I've been up to since August 13th. Learning and practicing how to survive.

My new soul sister Diana Nyad faced her life-threatening obstacles, including shark infested dark choppy waters, extreme fatigue with hydration and loss of nutrition, horrific bites and stings of jellyfish, all this and more without a shark cage, all because she had a dream that didn't die, a dream she kept alive. And she made it.

Later on the same day Diana answered questions and reflected on her dream come true. She enumerated three of her truths:

1. Never ever give up.
2. You're never too old to chase your dreams.
3. While this extreme effort may seem a solitary feat, the truth is it's very much a team effort.

Thank you Diana Nyad, 64 year old champion, extreme dreamer and new sister teacher of mine.

* * *

"That's beautiful, Mom," I said, "so encouraging." We talked more, then I read:

cmp, 9-3-13

"Unexpected Invitations"

Late last Friday, Donna Heald, the new Dean at Russell Sage College, called apologizing for the "incredibly short notice," but would I be "interested in teaching...."

Teaching? My interest peaked.

"Public Speaking.....the class starts Monday...."

This Monday?

"22 students...."

That's a lot for this sort of class.

"....it runs August 26 through December 6, then exams."

That's the whole fall, but I do need the money...

"... it pays....."

For 4 months of work? I graciously declined. "But please keep me in mind..."

Hanging up the phone, I felt conflicted. Do you want to teach this class, Col?

Yes! I called Donna back and accepted.

When I was young, all I wanted to be was a teacher. I ran a summer school for my younger siblings in the tool shed behind our house. In high school, though, one brief conversation with a guidance counselor about the "poor job market" for teachers at the time, led me in another direction, down another path.

Today, I have three decades of professional experience to mesh with my still-passionate love for teaching, which to me means to inspire. Perhaps with that unexpected invitation last Friday, Spirit pointed me in a new direction, a new path leading back to the work I loved from the start, from the tool shed to the ivory tower, finally happily *home*.

* * *

"I'm so glad you're teaching, Col," Mom said.

* * * * *

Week 41, September 11, 2013

Small Hands – Handle with Care

I picked up Mom at her apartment. Ever since the pace-maker heart scare last month, she has not felt safe driving. Her mobility has slowed to the point where she takes two or three steps, stops to catch her breath and strength, walks two or three more steps, then stops again. I find myself walking ahead, hoping she'll pick up the pace, in denial, refusing to accept the fact that she really cannot walk any faster.

We got a booth by the window at the Country View Diner. Our waitress, Mindy, was so happy to see my mother. Mindy always asks "how's your Mom doing?" when Columbus and I come here on Sundays for breakfast.

When I told Mindy about the book we're writing and how with today's installment she is now "officially in the book," Mindy's eyes glistened with joy.

"That's wonderful," she said. "I am a positive person, too. No matter what I've gone through in my life (leaving family in Vietnam to come here, divorce, raising three children alone) if I can find one good thing a day, that's what matters. If I can make one person smile, cheer someone up, that's what's important, right?"

"Right," Mom and I said in unison.

"We should do a signing here when our book is published, Mom."

"Sounds good to me," she said.

After lunch, I read first:

cmp, 9-11-13

Small Hands

Today is September 11, 2013, and no matter what happens on this day or on any other September 11th in the future, one particular September 11th, 9-11-01, the dark day of the terrorist attacks in NYC, will forever be engraved on our collective national memory.

On "that September 11th," I was giving my then baby goddaughter, Lauren, a bath in the kitchen sink. The phone rang and the tape machine recorded the shocked voice of my friend Paula Davenport from Florida sharing what she was watching live on CNN.

In that moment, my eyes landed on Lauren's tiny hand wrapped around my finger, so innocent and trusting. I snapped a mental photograph of her small hand.

The next morning, sitting at my blank computer screen, wanting to "do something".... we all wanted to "do something" and I am a writer so I wanted to write, I looked up and saw the framed poem my son, Connor, wrote in 2nd grade. He had traced his small hand, colored it with every crayon in the box, and then wrote a proud list of things that hand could do. "With this hand I can plant a seed. With this hand I can....."

I thought of Lauren's hand, and then Connor's hand.... and I typed:

"Your hands are small, but they do *big* things that make this a wonderful world."

That sentence became the first line in my picture book: *26 Big Things Small Hands Do* (Free Spirit). When visiting schools to speak, I smile at the banners, displays, booklets, even quilts of handprints and proud statements about what big things small hands can do, and I feel proud knowing that out of the darkness that was "that September 11th, I planted one bright new seed with this book that continues to blossom.

* * *

"Oh that's beautiful, Col," Mom said. "That's a lovely piece."

She handed me her paper. "I wrote about Camp Russell."

At those words, my heart clenched. I feel so sad for my Mom to be losing this place she loves so very much. The closing is this Saturday and because of her weak condition, Mom doesn't even feel strong enough to drive there one last time.

"What I really want to do is walk down the trail to the lake," she said, "but I know my legs aren't strong enough."

psm, 9-11-13

Handle With Care

Camp Russell is letting us wrap her up and hand her over to the next family of caretakers. After 13 years of cleaning her up, fixing her up, dressing her up, restoring her 80-some years of Adirondack splendor, it's time to say goodbye and that's almost impossible to do. The truth is we four sisters are aging and feeling the physical restrictions that come with the years, the financial constrictions that come with living on our social security or small pension. Mimi's still our baby (turned 70 this year) and while we've all done our part and we know what labors we've expended, it's certainly been my observation that Mim's effort has been the longest and most tireless to do Camp Russell. It was Mim back in 2000 who qualified to secure the mortgage in her name that gave us Camp Russell, and she's kept the books all this time.

Indeed everyone in this big family who has christened Camp Russell over the years with gifts, visits, celebrations and campkeeping (you know, like in housekeeping) knows that saying goodbye is not something easy or even possible to do. Once Camp Russell touches your heart she has captured you – and she doesn't let go.

(Col note: I'm crying here, but I try to be strong and positive for my Mom. How ironic that she is losing Camp Russell and I am losing Cape Cod, both in the same year.)

I have seven full journals in my own cursive started in 2001 in which I tell or try to tell some of the CR story, this labor of love. To say our blood, sweat, and tears are left here is only part of the thank-you note we send to her now. She's in our DNA. Those journals are a gift to be read by our loving children, grandchildren, brothers, cousins, not to forget sister Cindy in Tennessee whom we love too much to ever call our half sister.

It's a senior thing so I'm going to resist itemizing all the sisters' considerable health problems; but they are real. I am 75, trying to heal myself from a major and latest heart setback in August. Janie, 77 this year, is dealing with a knee replacement and serious complications attended to that surgery and she's doing her therapy so she can walk again. Virginia , 76 in Salem, while still managing to drive (she's been to CR several times this summer) is battling diabetes and all that goes with it. Mimi at 70 is no doubt the healthiest of the four of us, but even Mim knows and feels she isn't 45 or 50 anymore. Her bones let her know when she's overdone it, something she tends to do a little more than just now and then.

So much is going on in our troubled world as I see watching MSNBC and I have much to say about what our country is up to in Syria and a lot of other things. Like what are the lessons on this anniversary today of 9-11-2001? But we sisters here and now are being told it's time to wrap up Camp Russell, handle her with care -- tie and fasten her gently. And don't ever stop telling her beautiful story.

To be continued.

* * *

"Kinda sad, huh?" my mother said, making light of such a painful moment.

"I'm so sorry, Mom," I said.

"You were right there from the beginning with me on Camp Russell, Col," Mom said. "Remember how we packed a lunch and went to clean the screens and windows that first day? And you and Tony giving money to Mim and me for the down payment? And the stove you bought us and the kayak we named Willa....."

"We'll always stay connected to Camp Russell," I said. "My boys and I have already decided that we will go to back to Old Forge every summer for a night...stay in one of the motels in town...and visit Lake Tekini. Kevin and his family are on board, too, and I know Jerry will be as well."

Mom smiled. "That's nice. I hope so."

* * * * *

Week 42, September 17, 2013

Tag....You're It! – Absolutely a Visitor's Center

Mom was sitting on the bench outside the entrance to her apartment building patiently waiting when I arrived rushing late as usual to pick her up.

"What a beautiful day," she said.

We had planned on driving to Jose Malone's a Mexican-Irish

restaurant we love downtown, but it was after 1pm and I was starving and wanted to go someplace closer.

"How about that Middle Eastern place on 15th street," I suggested, surprised that I thought of it as I've never eaten there before.

"Ali Baba?" Mom said, equally surprised. "Oh, sure. That's a wonderful place."

A sunny table by the window was waiting for us.

I told Mom about the amazing experience I'd had on Sunday witnessing the ordination of the first female Catholic priest in the Capital Region.... Mary Theresa Streck... a mutual friend. "It was so joyful," I said. "The woman bishop from Rochester, all the women priests and deacons, smiling so happy on the altar. In the readings I learned that there were female disciples....Phoebe and Junia.... and others. Why hadn't I ever heard these names before? When they sang the litany of saints, they included peace and justice heroes such as Bishop Romero and Jay Murnane (Mary Theresa's beloved deceased husband, a former Catholic priest and beloved mentor friend of my mother's). "Oh, Mom, it was a glorious day."

"I wished I could have been there," she said. "I wrote to Mary Theresa."

Mom looked over the menu and decided right away. "I want the lamajun."

"What's that," I asked.

"Lamb pie."

When a man came to take our order, Mom told him, "I grew up just a few streets from here. There was an Armenian baker in our neighborhood. My mother would make ground lamb with spices and send us to him to cook it. He charged 3 cents a pie....."

The man clearly loved listening to my Mom. "I like your mother," he said to me.

He looked about my mother's age. I checked his left hand for a wedding ring.

I ordered a "small plate" -- roasted eggplant salad, humus, stuffed grape leaves.

A steaming hot-from-the oven loaf of Lavish (bread) dotted with sesame seeds was delivered "compliments of the house" (people love my Mom). We poked the bread with our forks to let the steam out, then tore off small pieces and dipped them into the dill yogurt sauce dressing. *Heaven.*

"The lamajun the baker in my neighborhood made was so thin you could roll it up," my Mom said. She smiled. "It's funny what you remember about your childhood."

"And it only cost 3 cents?" I said.

"Well, 10 cents if you bought a pie from him; 3 cents if he just baked it for you."

It was our best lunch yet.

"I feel my mother's spirit here," Mom said.

Our eyes met. I smiled.

"I do," Mom said, "really, I do."

"I believe you," I said. "That's wonderful."

"Why don't you read first," Mom said, and so I did.

cmp, 9-17-13

Tag....You're it!

Today the thrill of fall is in the air. I say "thrill" because at some random moment every September I feel this giddy childlike wave of excitement come over me. I can't mark it to the sight of something, like the first snowflake of winter.....or the first crocus of the spring.....although this morning a sweet orange maple leaf drifted past me as I jogged... it is more a "new school year" feeling of a fresh open slate where anything is possible. Today fall "tagged" me with hopefulness and I believe again.

The "muck and muddle" of summer has passed. Tony and I have agreed to remain apart....to continue on these new paths we've begun... and to try to be the best parent-partners we can be for our children, and the best friends we can be for each other.

Columbus moved in last weekend. And after all of my worries and toss-and-turn nights, I can happily report that it feels "right" – easy, comfortable, *good*.

It was a great decision to say "yes" to the unexpected invitation to teach at Russell Sage. I am *loving* this. My students are amazing. I feel so energized, like this is what I was born to do. I hope they'll offer me a full-time position there some day.

St. Joe hasn't worked his magic yet, but I have faith that the Cape house will sell soon. As my friend Krista McGrath (a three time beneficiary of the St. Joseph method of home selling) wrote to me: "It will happen in time..... God's time."

In the meantime, Columbus and I are headed out to the Cape for the weekend. I finally feel like I can just enjoy being on the Cape without needing to own a home there. I will always be "at home there" and, and as my Willa says, "nobody owns the ocean." (Sadly still no contract for a new Willa book yet.)

Fall is in the air. Tag....you're it....*what is good in your life today*?

"Oh that's great, Col," Mom said, and then she read:

psm, 9-17-13

Absolutely a Visitor's Center

Thank you to Debra Lockrow and John Cubit for your Pulse of the People of September 15 citing all the reasons why Troy needs a visitor's center. I couldn't agree more.

Being a young-at-heart senior, born here in 1938, I have memories galore -- childhood, teenage, young mother, on to becoming a grandmother, right up to these senior days here right now. I can go downtown – have a great desire to go downtown and walk my city's story again. It's not about bringing back yesterday; it's about bringing those beautiful memories right up to this moment when my city has come alive and young-at-heart again in this 21st century.

Of course we need a visitor's center. People need one central stop where they can walk in and see all that's new, all that's renovated, as well as all that's remembered. Of course our internet web world would let us scroll and access as we walk around inside the center and plan a stroll and let Troy tell her story—again. We have brand new shops in yesterday's grand old buildings, restaurants feeding us now as we sit and refresh ourselves in yesterday's elegance. Of Troy you could say this grand old lady is growing old, but as I see it is she is growing young and fresh and wants to show off again.

Of course we need a visitor's center. If there is a game board of Troy (and I seem to remember there was) the visitor's center is located right where it says Start Here. I bet I could even find a few very refined seniors who would love to welcome our visitors when they walk into this thanks-for coming- to-Troy visitor's center. It's right downtown.

⁂

"Mom, this is wonderful," I said. "You should definitely send this to Lisa Lewis (Editor of *The Record*).

As we gathered up to go, I gave Mom a copy of a feature story that had run in the *Times Union* about my sister-in-law Coll's aunt, Ellen McNulty, mayor of Green Island (and owner of McNulty Funeral Home) thinking she might like to read it and then pass along a copy to Colleen.

"Oh, good," Mom said, in a light joking way. "I need to talk with Ellen about my final party plans." (not sure Mom's exact words here...)

She laughed, so I laughed, too, keeping the moment light, but I thought about that all the way home.

⁂ ⁂

Fall

Week 43, September 24, 2013

Big Questions – Walking Meditation

Mom was waiting for me in front of her apartment building. She smiled when she saw me and began walking slowly toward my car, heavy totes in each hand -- one filled with personal belongings and things connected to our project, the other filled with all of her medications for an appointment with her heart doctor after our lunch meeting.

"Shall we try and find the Jamaican place?" I said.

"Sounds good," she said.

For months now my mother had been suggesting that we try out a new Jamaican restaurant in the North Central neighborhood down the hill from us. We didn't have an address so I took a chance at driving up 5th Avenue and within a few blocks we spotted the bright orange sign for "Hot Spot." As I turned the car around, we saw the Missing Link church where several months before we had gone to that community rally.

Inside Hot Spot, a warm, colorful, inviting space, Mom settled her things at a sunny table by the window and joined me at the counter to read the menu board.

I introduced us to the young woman waiting to take our order and told her about our book. She said she was the owner's niece. They were from St. Anne, Jamaica.

"Would it be okay if we put your name in the book," I asked.

"Sure," she said. "I'm Renee Mauzon," spelling out her last name for me.

Mom and I decided on the "Daily Lunch Special" – your choice of curried, fried, baked or jerk chicken, served with rice and peas, and either cabbage or plantains.

We chose the curried chicken, and when I asked whether Renee recommended the cabbage or plantains, she smiled and said, "We'll give you some of both." The entire bill, bottled drinks included, was less than $14. I put $5 in Renee's tip jar.

A few minutes later our hot savory meals were delivered.

"Absolutely delicious," Mom said.

"I *love this*," I said.

We both had enough to take half home for dinner. Well, no, in my case, my son Dylan scarfed down the leftovers within 5 minutes of my returning home. I took Dylan on a trip to Jamaica last year and he swears it was his "best vacation ever." I'd love to take him there again one day, perhaps as a 21st birthday gift.

"You read first, Col," Mom said.

cmp, 9-24-13

Big Questions

Dear Mom,

Last week when I gave you a copy of that story on Ellen McNulty, you said you needed to talk with her about your final party or parting plans. I forgot your exact words.

(Col note: I stopped reading here. "What did you call it, Mom?"

"I don't remember," she said, "but I think I said 'parting plans.'"

"I like *party* plans better," I said.)

Then I continued reading:

Well, we definitely will not be going to that party anytime soon, but it did get me thinking about how tremendously lucky I have been to have had so much quality, meaningful, soul-sharing time with you this year. We've made each week matter, Mom. We've done something important here which I hope will inspire others to do the same.

Too often people wait until a loved one is near death before they talk about what really counts. If our book has been about anything, it is about celebrating life while we are living, about speaking openly, now.

I still have some big questions, Mom. Perhaps you will answer them sometime.

Big Questions:

> Were you ever "in love" with someone after Dad?
>
> Did you want to find a new life partner?
>
> What did you love best about my father?
>
> When you were young, what did you want to be when you grew up?
>
> Any major life regrets?
>
> Any places you would love to visit?

(Col note: At this point my mother interrupted, "These are all questions for *me*?" You must be kidding me." I responded, "Just a line or two is all I was thinking. This is what came to me to write this week, Mom. You do what you want. That's up to you.")

I continued reading:

> Goals/dreams you still want to accomplish?
>
> If you could talk with any person from the past (no longer alive), who and why?
>
> If you could talk with anyone still living, who and why?
>
> What did you love most about your mother?
>
> What did you love most about your father?
>
> If you could relive one day in your life, which one would it be?
>
> Thoughts about death?
>
> Thoughts about God?
>
> Heaven/hereafter?
>
> Your happiest life moments.
>
> Your saddest life moments.
>
> What line would you have inscribed on your headstone?
>
> What do you want your legacy to be (be remembered for)?
>
> Something people might be surprised to know about you.

Any secrets you are willing to share?

Your most prized possessions?

Your best prayer?

Thanks for considering this, Mom.

Love you,

Col

"That's beautiful, Col," my mother said. "It gives me much to think about. And thanks for reminding me about calling Ellen McNulty."

That was certainly not my intention with this piece, but I let it go. "Your turn, Mom," I said, checking my watch as I remembered she had a doctor's appointment.

Then, despite the fact that her appointment began in twenty minutes and we still had to drive there, Mom read her piece in the same slow, measured, lilting way she always reads aloud..... totally in the moment, relishing every word. And although I've heard my mother read aloud countless times, today it struck me how much *joy* it brings her to *read aloud*... and how I cannot wait to be sitting next to her at events and listen as she reads excerpts from *our* book to an audience. Just wait until they hear my Mom.

psm, 9-24-13

Walking Meditation

I was meditating the other day here on my couch, just taking a moment to calm my cluttered mind. So I breathed deeply, closed my eyes and let myself travel down to that soul place, the place of silent meditation. After about five minutes I brought myself back to what I call my real world. And there it was; the single word the Holy Spirit had left me with: *Walking.* That's right; my conscious thought was just simply *walking*.

I took pen in hand as I always do (it's how I think out loud) and started writing down my *walking* thoughts: (Right now writing this I stop and go looking for those *walking* notes and I'm frustrated because I can't find them.) But I remember it was a short list, maybe half a dozen walking things, things like: *take a walk, walk to the door, walk over here, walk over the block, walk down the street, walk to the park, walk with me, walk away* – things like that.

I know I've said here in Writing Us Right and elsewhere, ad nausea; how I'm 75, have this healing heart, etc. etc. One of the things I'm supposed to do every day is *walk.* Truth is I've made more excuses why I haven't or didn't or couldn't walk; more excuses than there are times when I actually have taken a walk.

One of the childhood scoldings that came from a teacher, a parent, or other authority figure in my growing up life sounds like: "Get up and walk on your own two feet." Imprints of memory show me walking everywhere, like when at maybe four, too young to be running (walking) away with my doll carriage and best friend Sally, or, walking over to the vacant lot behind our Beman Park house; walking to the store for my mother; and later, when I was a thin and pretty teenager of 14 going on 15 and walking downtown, hand in hand with my first love Jerry, then over the Congress St. bridge to Hank's in Watervliet to go dancing (people would say like Fred Astaire and Ginger Rogers), and then walking back over the bridge to Troy and all the way home. And, later of course I would walk down the aisle, then walk my babies, and later finally getting a social conscience in my early forties, walking in peace demonstrations. all the time *walking, walking, walking.*

The longer I live the more I understand that my life is a walking miracle. Thank you, Spirit, for whispering to me; and once again for letting me see that walking is part of who I am, indeed is what I am. I hear you saying, "Come and walk with me." It's a win- win meditation.

* * *

When Mom finished reading, I noticed people at neighboring tables smiling in appreciation of my mother's message. "That's wonderful, Mom" I said. "Did people really say that you and Dad were like Fred Astaire and Ginger Rogers?"

"Oh yes," she said. "We were the most popular dancers of our time."

* * * * *

Week 44, October 1, 2013

Resurrecting Autumn – Smiling at Church

My mother looked so pretty sitting on the bench in front of her apartment building, a festive leaf-patterned scarf around her neck. "What a gorgeous day," she said.

"Couldn't be more beautiful," I said.

After discussing restaurant possibilities – we only have nine weeks left and want to "spread the love" as much as possible, we set course for Carol's on Pawling Avenue, passing by stately old homes my Nana cleaned when she first emigrated here from Ireland, up past the sprawling campus of the Emma Willard School.

Our waitress, Casey, was cheerful and accommodating. Mom ordered the chicken Caesar salad wrap; I opted for the grilled veggie. Mary Ann Giordano, a dear friend of my Aunt Sue Spain and Aunt Bett Phoenix, came to our table to tell my mother how "wonderful" she looked and to say how much she enjoyed my book, *Dreamsleeves*. "Write another book about Troy," she said. Mom read first:

psm, 10-1-13

Resurrecting My Autumn

It's that time of the year again, autumn is here; and as autumn always does here in the Northeast, it comes to us in living color. On a personal level today, I think of myself, my own life as being in my autumn time.

Mim drove us over Route 7 to Bennington this past Sunday to see the changing of the season. Summer will say goodbye, winter will say ready or not here I come, but on this Sunday my eyes feasted on God's spectacular fall wonder and I had a born again experience. Feeling reborn when you're 75 and healing slowly from the latest breakdown of my heart; teaching my feet to carry me again – bringing all those years and all this healing into the miracle of this Autumn Sunday, well, indeed, that was for me being born again and it was knowing a resurrection.

Autumn's spectacular beauty on Sunday was the gift that gave me new life. Poets and writers and photographers and artists have ever tried to capture autumn's unspeakable beauty. And they know they've fallen short. And like me they will keep trying. God has opened the heavens and poured out heaven on earth under a sun-filled blue and white clouds sky using a Supreme brush and palette of colors beyond human description.

It's just God's gift on this day: every shade of orange, gold, scarlet red, brown, all dancing a celebration love song before my eyes. Something was reborn in me. My heart opened and I felt the healing. God was saying something like "Remember this, a preview of heaven to come and it's yours today right here on earth."

Inside the barnlike bakery gift shop I chose my autumn bounty, at least what I could carry. I wanted to and would have taken a small round pumpkin but I'm ever grateful for just feasting my eyes on those orange and off-white gems in small medium and large. What I could carry: a bag of apples -- six different choices and I chose Macoun; then from several bread choices a fresh baked loaf of (do you believe this) Sunflower Seed Wheat, and finally, of course, apple cider donuts.

When autumn comes in regal living color you know you've breathed in and looked upon a miracle. I knew that Sunday -- in its entire autumn splendor, I knew the feeling of being reborn and the feeling of living my autumn resurrection.

* * *

"That's beautiful, Mom," I said, "so uplifting."

"Thanks, Col."

"I hope to get to Vermont soon," I said. "Tony and I used to go every fall."

"I remember," Mom said, and then I read this:

cmp, 10-1-13

Smiling at Church

"Thank you for smiling," someone often says to me after Mass at Our Lady of Victory Church when I am the lector for one of the scripture readings.

I appreciate these comments, but *why wouldn't I smile?*

It is such a tremendous honor, something to be joyful about.

I love it when I get a reading with an encouraging line or even just a happy word or two because then I can smile more. If I get a dreary piece, the only two chances I'll get to smile are when I first make eye contact, acknowledging the congregation, and then at the end with, "This is the word of the Lord," and so I make those moments count.

People come to church with heavy hearts and painful baggage. You can see it in their eyes. Fears about their health or the health of a loved one, grief over a recent death, worries about their partners, children, parents, the loss of a job, a marriage in turmoil, addictions, betrayals, bills. We come to seek comfort, to feel a bit more "okay."

If I can help a bit with a simple smile, why would I choose to be somber?

Two Sundays ago I experienced a singular joyful celebration when Mary Theresa Streck was officially ordained the first Catholic woman priest in our region. The ceremony, at one of my old churches, The First Unitarian Universalist Society of Albany, was packed to the rafters. Columbus and I found seats up on the balcony amongst photographers and camera operators from local television stations.

I was so excited to be there, me, nearly 55 years a Catholic and never having seen a woman *right where Jesus would have wanted her*, up front like his beloved Mary Magdelene, equally as important as Peter, Paul, Luke and John. I peered down as the line of white-robed women – bishop, visiting priests, two women who would be ordained deacons and Mary Theresa who would become a priest today, processed toward the altar. When they turned to greet the assembly, my eyes filled with tears.

Every single one of them was *smiling* --- big radiant jubilant smiles that warmed the room like suns. No, not sons, daughters.

Jesus never said women couldn't be priests – men said that.

They were wrong.

It was an unforgettably joyous afternoon in that church.

And everyone, *everyone*, was smiling.

* * * * *

Week 45, October 8, 2013

My Almost Education – Anticipation

At Sweet Sue's on River Street, we ordered the 16 bean and kale soup and a ham and fancy-cheese croissant sandwich with a side salad of farm fresh greens and assorted tomatoes, then went outside to claim a sunny table under a red umbrella.

"I haven't been to this part of River Street in years," Mom said, admiring the freshly painted grand old buildings, many now housing interesting retail stores. "I could spend a day just going in and out of all these shops," she said.

Our waitress, Emmy, came out often to check on us.

"This is the best soup I've ever had," I said.

Later, the owner, chef Susan Dunkel, came out to say hello, clearly pleased that we were enjoying her food and restaurant so much. Mom read first:

psm, 10-8-13

My Almost Education

I'm thinking a lot about my life, probably because I've reached

75 and despite quite a few crises of the heart over the years I'm still here. When I pondered something to write about I came up with how I almost went to college but didn't. Well it was hit or miss -- and for earning that bachelor's degree, it was a miss.

My inquisitive mind has always loved the classroom. Back in the 1950's when I started high school there were only two choices as to what curriculum we could study for four years. You either took a College Entrance course or you took a Business course. In those days you were expected to know as a freshman what you would be – for girls it was a nurse, a teacher, or a nun. Otherwise you wouldn't be going to college so your alternative was to take a Business course; that way you'd be able to get a job as soon as you graduated. That's what I did and did it with honors in Secretarial Practice. But there was always this feeling of not being quite as good as that half of my class who were preparing for college.

I've gone beyond feeling sorry for myself about never graduating from college. But I've always had this strong urge, this longing to learn, to answer the questions that were inside me. Even when I was totally caught up in the chaos and the demands of my life -- my husband's addiction, my struggle to help my children , I knew there was something I had missed. Occasionally when I let myself dream I pictured myself sitting in a classroom, listening to the wise words of a learned professor, completing myself.

I excelled in my chosen field, I was a good secretary. And I think it was in the early 1980s when I saw in the Albany paper a night course being offered in communications at Albany Business College and I took the course. I remember looking at a handout in class and seeing in bold print, "the pen is mightier than the sword." Later I took out a loan and took night courses at The College of Saint Rose, one course at a time, always after finishing my work day and with children waiting for me at home. I remember a religion course I took because the name caught my eye: The Christian Failure. I took other courses in Spanish, Public Speaking, Expository Writing and Research Techniques, Sociology,

Journalism, etc. (Somewhere in this apartment of paper memories I could probably find the records of what I took at Saint Rose and when.)

At one point I became interested in pursuing the college's newly offered Experienced Adult Program, where you could earn college credits by documenting learned life skills that conformed to specific course requirements in their catalog. I remember Professor Ann Sheridan who encouraged me to keep going and complete my portfolio which was well in the works. But I caved in, emotionally, physically; this depressed body just couldn't do it all and I never completed enough of the EAP to earn the credits I would have been awarded.

I've always had a flair for the Spanish language; took 2 years in high school, again at St. Rose, once a night course at Troy High. Always the student, always on fire, and always part time. (When we gather for a special meal, my family asks me to say the grace before meals in Spanish: I gladly offer: *Damos gratias a Dios, por la comida, la salud, la familia y la communidad. Oremos for paz en el mundo, y en el corazon. Amen.)*

So my almost education is still with me. I'm still going strong; the books are always open, I'm still taking notes, and I'm going to keep going chapter and verse until I'm satisfied that I've earned my degree.

* * *

I choked up as Mom read this. She is the smartest person I know with an insatiable appetite for learning. She would have graduated with honors from any college. Perhaps it's not too late. Maybe this could be the next goal when our book is finished?

We talked a bit and then I read:

cmp, 10-8-13

Anticipation

I love October.

Here at my desk as I type, a refreshing breeze blows in. The sky is royal blue. The trees in Frear Park are dazzling divas in pumpkin, gold, and garnet gowns. I take a sip of warm ginger tea and breathe in the aroma of an apple-scented candle.

Life is good. *Thank you.* I am abundantly blessed.

Lately each day seems to bring a new invitation to move toward joy. The teaching's going well, the writing's going well, my sons are good, Columbus and I are good, my Mom is happier than I've seen her in months. My family is coming for Thanksgiving and I'm happily anticipating all of that -- leafing through cookbooks, rounding up runners for the Troy Turkey Trot, planning how to comfortably fit 16 for dinner in my small house, picturing how I will set the table, linens, flowers, candles...

Anticipation of a happy occasion is a very good thing. Each time we imagine and look forward, we get to experience a bit of the happy warm pleasure, *the joy*, countless times before the actual day, and as my girl Sunny would say, "it doesn't cost a cent."

Last Sunday, Columbus dug up a patch of ground along the deck outside the kitchen door window and we planted pockets of daffodil bulbs, 5 or 6 to a circle. Such ugly things, those bulbs – hard to imagine the frilly yellow beauty, perfume, and cheer to come when they bloom next spring. I know that many times throughout the cold winter ahead, I will smile in anticipation of that.

Week 46, October 15, 2013

Following Francis – Sunday Mornings

We went to the Recovery Grill at the Hilton on Hoosick Street for lunch.

Seated in a comfortable booth, I noted the pool table we had passed at the entrance and said perhaps we could come here with my boys. Mom loved playing pool with her grandsons at Slickers restaurant near Camp

Russell in Old Forge. We ordered wrap sandwiches, chicken salad and turkey with avocado. Two friends of my mother's, Maureen Noonan and Caroline Smith, really cool, fun ladies, stopped by to say hello.

"I've decided to be positive about Francis (the new pope)," Mom said, then read:

psm, 10-14-13

Following Francis

I'm an old Catholic girl and I've been given these 75 years to leave my footprint and I'm still asking myself, "What's the point?" Could it be that Pope Francis is on the scene at this time to bring me back to square one? Francis is on my mind.

Last night CNN did an update marking the first six months of his papacy. Just six months as the titular head of 6.5 billion Catholics around the one world – and if I'm sure of anything it's that Francis has my attention; and I think the attention of much of the world. It may be irreverent to say Francis is a rock star, but the point is made -- where Francis goes the paparazzi and the cameras go. And so do the little people who are invited to come out of their hiding, their despair, and have been given a shred of hope.

Where I'm coming from at this stage of the game poses another question in my searching mind: "Who cares?" I'll speak for myself when I say I care. Love has not yet overcome evil, the innocent still suffer, and as a communicator I believe that we're supposed to be paying attention, be about the business of doing the right thing. Francis has been given a starring role on the world scene. You will see him all over the news and print media. I hope we (I) don't get too caught up in the hype and lose the point of Francis' presence. People are watching as evil is still able to trample goodness. With Francis, I feel a good sized measure of hope that this man of my generation and my religion is in the world spotlight and is showing us a way. Could it be that his presence is making the powers that be in Rome a tad uncomfortable? Who is this Francis, stirring up the waters of power and complacency?

I can only speak for myself but in saying that I know I speak for many. Francis wants us to seek and find the forgotten, the chastised, the unforgiven, the cold and hungry, the needy. And guess what? That's what my faith has ever told me. That's exactly what Jesus was about.

So at the end of my little sermon to myself, I return to my questions which I think Francis has answered. "What's the point?" "Who cares?" This wise man of my faith, this man of my generation has the world spotlight and is walking a walk that speaks of loving the least and coming out -- and to paraphrase the Good News -- not hiding your lamp under a basket. Francis is out there using his intelligent mind, his warm, loving heart, his aging and still active hands and feet, and using the example of his namesake Francis of Assisi to point us in the right direction.

The lowly wait in joyful hope. Francis is a leader to follow.

cmp, 10-15-13

Sunday Mornings

Although we are different in many ways, one of the great things Columbus and I have in common is that on Sunday mornings we both love to go to church and out to breakfast after. Sometimes we go to Metropolitan New Testament Baptist where Columbus sings in the male chorus; other weeks it's Our Lady of Victory where I lector. Sometimes we opt for more sleep, but still go out for breakfast. It's become a tradition.

The first two years we were together we would try different restaurants, but when Columbus began calling the Country View Diner "our place," it soon began to feel like that. Now we go there every Sunday. We know the waitresses' names – Mindy, Robin, Debi, Karen -- and when we leave, the hostess says, "See you next week!"

Columbus orders what I would consider a Christmas morning breakfast... Belgian waffles with fruit topping and whipped cream, scrambled eggs with cheese, sausage and bacon, home fries and toast. I usually get Egg-beater scrambled eggs with Canadian bacon and a slice of dry wheat toast, or, when I'm feeling reckless, I'll ask for a pancake, "no butter" and pull out a tiny container of sugar-free maple syrup from my purse. Columbus shakes his head and laughs. Our waitress brings more coffee.

I'll take out the Jumble (scrambled word game) from the Sunday paper and two pens and we'll try to solve it before our food arrives. When it does, Columbus bows his head and quietly prays: "Lord we thank you for this food we are about to receive, and bless the hands that prepared it, in Jesus' name we pray, Amen."

* * * * *

Week 47, October 23, 2013

Birthday Cards – Remember the Forgotten

My mother saw her heart doctor yesterday. "Not good news." She is still experiencing atrial-fibrillation and "they are concerned." On Friday she is scheduled for two out-patient tests at Samaritan Hospital, an Esophageal Echo where they insert a tube down the windpipe to see if there are clots, and if that test goes well, a Cardio-Version Shock Test to try to jolt the heart into a normal rhythm.

We met for tea at 3:00 pm at Mom's. On the little table by the window, there was a tiny ceramic bowl for each of us filled with mixed nuts and dried fruits with a wrapped square of Ghirardelli's dark chocolate on top, along with our favorite pink Dorothy Parker "millionaire" napkins. Mom was wearing a pin with this quote:

I always wanted to be somebody
but now I realize I should have
been more specific.

"Oh that's great," I said, and we laughed.

"That's one of Stanley's pins (manager of Market Block Books)," she said, still laughing, walking back to her kitchen to read aloud a few other priceless quotes on refrigerator magnets she had purchased at her favorite bookstore in the world.

"Why don't you read first," Mom said, and so I did:

cmp, 10-23-13

Birthday Cards

I turned 55 last Saturday, October 19th, and for the first time in my life, no one sang "Happy Birthday to you...." and there was no cake. That was totally my fault. Columbus and I were in Indianapolis attending the wedding of his son, CJ, and I had pleaded with Columbus beforehand to please not even mention that it was my birthday as I wanted the focus to be totally on CJ and his bride, Desiree.

But still.... no card, no song, no cake? A candle stuck in a donut maybe?

There were phone calls from my sons and text messages from my friends, and when we got back to Troy, lovely cards, presents, and dinners out. Of all these gifts, the ones I will cherish most are the handwritten sentiments on the birthday cards.

When my boys were little, I taught them that homemade cards were always better than Hallmark. I encouraged (they might say "required"☺) them to make special occasion cards for family members and to "write three lines ... something nice."

"You never need to buy me anything for my birthday," I'd say to them, and still do today, "but I would love a card with a few lines from you."

Among my most treasured possessions are the cards my sons have made for me on Valentine's Day, Mother's Day, and birthdays over the years. I keep every single one.

Like this Mother's Day card Dylan made for me when he was 8 years old:

"To Mom, the one I love.
The one who cares about me.
The one who I'll be proud of when she's famous.
The one who tells me to write and read.
I think that's important because when I grow up
I want to have an intelligent discussion with someone just like my Mom.
P.S. Happy Mother's Day.
Love, Dylan

Yesterday, this same son, now 19, a tall grown handsome man, gave me a Hallmark card, but added his own heartfelt personal message:

"I love you Mom.
Happy Birthday!
With age comes wisdom; and so I hope for you the ability
to make any life decision
carefully and joyfully,
wholeheartedly and joyously,
and always with
Love."

❧ ❧ ❧

"I love that boy," Mom said. "This is beautiful, Col. I'm sorry I didn't get to talk to you on your birthday. I thought of you all day long. I even started to write you a poem. It's around here someplace. And we'll celebrate, I promise, when I get this heart thing settled."

We talked about her upcoming procedures and family stuff, then Mom read:

psm, 10-23-13

Remember the Forgotten

My prayer this morning is to remember those young souls who in their innocence have suffered at the hands of hundreds (more like thousands) of ordained clergy in my church in this country and throughout the world.

I was gifted last night because a friend (Martha Walsh) cared enough to call me to see if I wanted to go with her and our dear friend Mary Jane Smith to hear a talk at a Methodist church in Albany. Thank God I put my selfish worries about my upcoming heart tests aside and said yes. The Holy Spirit was speaking and I was there to hear.

The speaker was Fr. Tom Doyle, J.C.D. a world renowned canon lawyer. His talk was entitled, "The Unfinished Business of Clergy Sex Abuse." Among his many credentials are at least five master's degrees and a doctorate. Father Doyle -- who by the way squirms at being called Father because he says the word wrongly places the priesthood on a pedestal -- he's still in good standing in the church which means Rome hasn't thrown him out though they would love to silence him. He is a brilliant canon lawyer who has testified all over the United States and throughout the world in defense of young (mostly young men now no longer young) who at last have gotten their day in civil court. He stands strong and speaks for young souls whose lives have been torn apart because they trusted a priest who was supposed to be caring for their spiritual wellbeing and instead was molesting them.

It was nothing I hadn't heard or read before. So why bring it up now? Well Tom believes that as a people of God we have never really put this scandal where it belongs – right up front – right from the pulpit. We have never really acknowledged how much those injured on our watch need our ongoing love, compassion and support. Time wise, not since the early eighties when a 10-year old abused boy in Louisiana (I think it was) had the courage to speak out but was publicly chastised have we as a people of God tried to wipe our slate clean. We've said we are sorry but we would not have done so had the scandal not become visible, erupting on page 1 news of The Boston Globe.

Our speaker, Tom, acknowledged that once the scandal was out the patriarchy/hierarchy, many contrite and well-meaning, strove to make amends. Structures were set in place to prevent such wrongdoing ever again.

Father Doyle noted, however, and wanted us to reflect on the truth that last night he was not speaking in a Catholic church; and that's because he in fact is never allowed to speak in any Catholic church. His voice and other voices who speak out on this our horrendous scandal are mainly silenced in the church. On the other hand there has been a huge effort on damage control (big corporations with lots of money can do that). Let's focus on what will make us look good again. We are after all people of God.

The truth is we are all the children of God. At the Q&A one Albany woman, a mother whose child was molested by a priest spoke of her heart being broken at seeing her child broken, his own heart shattered. She's still a Catholic and speaks out at every opportunity because she no longer can trust any priest; this is a woman who taught in Catholic school and looked up to the priests like so many of us.

Another young man (looked 30-something) identified himself as a survivor of priestly abuse and thanked Fr. Doyle for being a strong and supportive voice, something too lacking in the church. Fr. Doyle paid homage with a warm hug, telling the young man that he as survivor was the hero, the courageous voice. (The young man later told Mary Jane and me his abuser was a brown-robed Franciscan priest from this diocese who used to take the boys on camping trips.)

In my scripture memory Jesus says something like "Let the little ones come to me and suffer them not." Well the little ones came, and God forgive us, they were abused beyond belief and have suffered. Many of them still walk among us, trying to live a wholesome life despite their brokenness. So do many of the guilty ones, garbed in black cassock and Roman collar (and as Tom points out) carrying their Latin breviary they can't even translate.

We need to know that making amends must be a lifetime effort and the children need to know that God loves them and protects them. And that we as God's people have not forgotten the least among us.

⁂

"This is so powerful Mom," I said. "Thank you for sharing this."

Col's Note: 10-25-13 GREAT NEWS!! --- Both heart tests went well. And **not one mention of depression** in weeks. Hooray !!!!!!

* * * * *

Week 48, October 31, 2013

A New Direction – The Old Ball Game

"Happy Halloween!" we greeted each other as I picked Mom up outside her apartment building. A cloudy day, it had just begun to drizzle.

"I feel sorry for the trick-or-treaters," Mom said. Children from nearby School 18 would be coming to Conway Court at 3:00 "to show off their costumes" and receive treat bags from Conway residents. "I hope it stops raining for their sake by then," she said.

We decided on the Knotty Pine for lunch. After we ordered our sandwiches, tuna fish and a turkey Reuben, my mother took out a funny hat and glasses she had worn to the Halloween luncheon at Conway Court the previous day. "It was fun," she said.

"I wish I had a picture of you," I said. "Maybe you could put them on after lunch and I'll take one." I thought about that first Halloween in Troy after my separation, how lonely and sad I felt, and how my Mom showed up to surprise me wearing a funny blue wig and dark glasses still smelling like chlorine from her swim at the YWCA up the street. She used to swim there a few times a week with her dear friend Mary Jane Smith. I pray my Mom will regain her health again, get back to swimming and walking again.

We talked about my class at Russell Sage and Mom's upcoming appointments. "It seems as if that's all I do is go to doctor's offices," she said.

We took out our pieces and I read first:

cmp, 10-31-13

A New Direction

St. Joe finally stepped up his game. My Cape Cod realtor called yesterday. "I have good news for you," she said. "We'll be getting an offer this weekend."

From a financial point of view, I am relieved. On a personal level, I thought I would feel sad, but, so far, I'm okay. Cape Cod will always be a part of me. My heart will forever swell at the site of that roller coaster bridge. But at this stage in my life--perhaps turning 55, perhaps because Columbus and I are so happy together and someday it would be nice to have a get-away- place that was "ours"—I'm ready for a new direction. The Cape is so tied to my three decades with Tony, 30 years of memories.

Last year, Columbus surprised me with a little trip to Maine. It was the first time I'd ever been. It was beautiful. A few months back I was quoted in a Times Union feature story about how for a great many people who live in the Capital (Albany, NY) region, there comes a point on the highway where roughly half choose "495 South" toward Cape Cod and the other half choose "495 North" heading toward Maine.

Perhaps now it is time for a new direction. Perhaps North, perhaps Maine.

My dear college friend Nancy Davison always raved about Maine. Two of my favorite writers, May Sarton (deceased) and Stephen King (very much alive) are Maine people. Columbus and I had such a good time there, the ocean, quaint towns, a more laid-back vibe than the Cape. I'm thinking Maine sounds like a fine new direction.

⁂ ⁂ ⁂

"I'm surprised, Col," Mom said. "Maine is so far away. I thought you and Columbus were talking about finding a place on a lake, somewhere not too far."

"We still are," I said. "We love the idea of a lake place."

"You should talk to Judy Rancourt," Mom said (the wonderful realtor who found my Troy house). "Judy would find you a great place."

We chatted a bit more, and then Mom read her piece:

psm, 10-31-13

The Old Ball Game

A love of baseball has been one of my things since childhood and continues today. This week I watched most of the World Series. Last night The Boston Red Sox beat the St. Louis Cardinals at Fenway Park to become the 2013 World Champions.

For me, you could say I grew up hearing and singing in my head (and occasionally out loud) this old refrain:

Take me out to the ball game,
Take me out with the crowd,

I know my dad was a many-lettered athlete at Troy High in the 1920s and later went on to play semi-pro baseball locally, before marriage and kids and Army and all that ended his athletic career. He loved the game and I must have inherited his genes. When we were kids and there was a major league game on the radio or later on TV, my dad was tuned in and we knew we had better not bother him.

When I was in St. Peter's grammar school, probably 11 or 12, I got to play softball which I understood as the same as baseball but with a softer ball. The area where we played was down in the vacant lot on River Street that belonged to what was then Cluett's shirt factory, a very large employer, home of the Sanforized shirt. (That's why we're called The Collar City.). Playing softball down at Cluett's (now Hedley's, still big business and the current leased quarters of City Hall) is one of my most cherished childhood memories, even though it was probably only for one or two seasons.

In those days baseball was America's most popular sport. I knew famous names like Joe DiMaggio, Mickey Mantle, Stan Musial, Leo Durocher, Babe Ruth.

Buy me some peanuts and Cracker Jacks,
I don't care if I ever get back,

And later in the 1970s when I was a busy young mother, the Pittsburgh Pirates would become my favorite team and Roberto Clemente my favorite player. The way this happened (I know I've told my children and grandchildren over and over!), is not a family secret. I was holding my newborn infant Danny Murtagh (September 10, 1971) and we were watching the 1971 World Series. To our big surprise we learned the manager of the Pirates was an Irishman and his name was Danny Murtagh. I remember the camera panning the dugout and we saw Dan's namesake and he looked like he could have (must have) been a family relative. He looked so much like my father-in-law, Mark Murtagh, who had died in 1962 so only my firstborn, Coleen, ever got to know him. That 1971 World Series did it: The Pittsburgh Pirates became my team -- still is -- and Danny Murtagh, their famous manager, we unofficially 'adopted' into our own Murtagh family.

So let's root, root, root for the home team,
If they don't win it's a shame...

When I became a single mother in 1980 I checked into Little League for Jerry, Dan and Kevin as soon as they reached an age when all three of them could play on the same team. (Baseball, nor any competitive sport had ever been offered or taught to them and to me that was a loss to be corrected.) I'm grateful to a good man, Ron Martone, now deceased who was coaching in Beman Park and took my sons under his father-like wing. Jerry, the oldest of the trio of Murtagh kids was never comfortable playing; he did his best but it wasn't his game. I would feel so badly for him when he would strike out. Dan and Kev on the other hand took to the game and both played very well.

Back to this week, I rooted for the underdog St. Louis Cardinals (my style always to root for the underdog) but history will show that the Red Sox win was just what Boston needed. It had been a very heartbreaking and painful year since the terrorist massacre at the Boston Marathon.

Baseball remains for me America's best sport. The Red Sox are to be celebrated, having gone in their own words, "from worst to first". And a healing city is comforted and has something to celebrate. Remember, win or lose,

So it's one, two, three strikes you're out
At the old ball game.

Save me a seat.

⁂ ⁂ ⁂

"I *love* this, Mom," I said. "It's personal yet loaded with history and current events. You are such a great writer."

"Thanks, Col."

Later, after I'd driven Mom home, I felt badly remembering that I'd forgotten to take a photo of her in her funny Halloween hat and glasses. Next year, for sure.

⁂ ⁂ ⁂ ⁂ ⁂

Week 49, November 6, 2013

Count My Vote – Laughter

We drove up Hoosick Street to Mocha Blend. As we placed our lunch orders, I recalled the first time I came here. It was the spring of 2008. My marriage was ripping apart and a separation was imminent. I was in a panic state trying to figure out where I would live and my mom offered to introduce me to a realtor named Judy Rancourt. "She's a *wonderful* person," Mom said.

Judy and I met for coffee here. I can still picture her compassionate smile and warm blue eyes, head nodding with understanding as she let me pour out my pain like she had all the time in the world to listen... how she gave me hope by sharing the story of her own journey with me...and then, and only then, did we talk about real estate. In short order, Judy found just the perfect house here for me in Troy -- not at all like the dream specs I had given her – "I want a colonial with a big front porch and a fireplace." This was a ranch, no porch, no fireplace – but it was perfect in ways I could not have imagined. Sort of the way God works.

Mom and I talked about plans for Thanksgiving. When our waitress, Amber, delivered our Panini sandwiches (which were delightful), I asked her to take our photograph. We told her about our book.

"That sounds wonderful!" Amber said.

I shared with my mother how much I loved teaching my students at Sage and how I would miss them. Mom said she got the "go ahead" from her doctors to drive and how her sister Mimi was taking her out for a "driving lesson" to help her gain confidence again. My Aunt Mimi is so good like that.

Mom read first:

psm, 11-5-13

Count My Vote

Well it's Election Day, so no surprise I'll go on a bit about voting. Yes, I exercised my citizen's right, my duty, and my privilege today. Logistically, it was no big effort; my building was the polling place for my district. It took no more effort than pushing the elevator button from my fifth floor apartment down to the first floor community room. (I hope this convenience was not the only reason I got myself out, but it certainly didn't hurt.)

I have my dad's genes for being political, for being opinionated; yes, you might say for being a political animal. I grew up hearing my father expound on all things political so I, too, always had thoughts and opinions

-- what party I leaned toward, who would I vote for and who would I definitely not. And, like today, what proposition needed my yes or no.

And what about all the pre-election campaigning? For the last month I've been up to here -- the everyday mailings upon mailings, and they looked expensive printed in full color. And the endless phone calls, including the voice of Governor Cuomo sharing his own opinion about the casino proposition. And the signs and posters covering lawns and buildings all over town. To say the least it was overkill, more than a little annoying.

I wasn't always so strong about voting. When I was just a young married I remember clearly going to register for the first time with my husband. I let him run things in those days and he told me not to check either Democrat or Republican, just leave it blank so his customers wouldn't know.

For many years that bothered my conscience, making me feel I was not quite fully participating. We didn't talk politics much at home in my early married years but I could always tell where my husband stood. It had to do with what was good for business. I also remember back in the sixties my Irish Catholic mother-in-law who was thirty years older saying that JFK was the only Democrat she had voted for since FDR. That of course was more about being Irish and Catholic and less about loyalty to one party.

So many decades have gone by and I have never again taken what I see as a cop-out. I vote my conscience. The best thing for me about voting is its privacy; nobody should know and nobody does know how you have voted. The privacy of the voting booth is one of the best, if not the best, guarantee about living in this wealthy, powerful, often less than perfect United States of America.

It's regretful that so many people never exercise their right to vote. I heard one of my co-residents being asked whether he had voted. His response? "No way, they're all a bunch of crooks, every one of them."

Now it's the morning after Election Day. As I was watching post-election wrap-ups on CNBC's Morning Joe, I was agreeing 100% with one of the guests, a Republican strategist. All the guests are asked at the end of every the show: "What, if anything did you learn today?" His answer: "After all is said and done, the people have the last word."

I agree 100% with the Republican strategist. Count my vote.

* * *

"I love this, Mom!"

"Thanks, Col."

"I shook President Kennedy's hand when his motorcade came through South Troy when I was little, right? At least that's what Dad always told me."

"That sounds right," Mom said.

Caroline Kennedy and I share connections...we're both authors, raised Catholic, long ties to Cape Cod, and I once shook her father's hand.

"What did you write about?" Mom asked.

"Laughter," I said, and we laughed.

cmp, 11-6-13

Laughter

We are so lucky to have funny people in our midst. I immediately think of Ellen DeGeneres. When I watch her on TV, before she even says a word, just by the delighted expression on her face, I know she's excited to make us laugh, that she's going to have fun with this and we will too. And I *love* how Ellen gets everyone dancing. I join in from my living room. I would love to dance on her show. Gotta add that to the bucket list.

I think of my mega-talented sister, improvisational comic Noreen Mahoney, founder of "Shirley You Must be Joking!" and "Say Anything." When I'm in the audience at one of Nor's shows, my face just about explodes I am smiling and laughing so hard. "That's my *sister*!" I want to shout. "Isn't she amazing?!?!"

Humor runs in the family. Our Dad, Jerry Murtagh, was a first-class joke teller. When we six siblings get together, Michael, Nor, Jerry, Dan,

Kevin, and I, it's a non-stop laughter fest – them, not me. I am, hands-down, the least funny of the bunch.

My assignment to my Russell Sage public speaking class last Thursday was to come prepared to deliver a joke or very short funny story. As it was Halloween, I brought in bags of candy as prizes for the top three "audience favorites" and little packets of Smarties candies for all. I was so proud of my students, how they rose to the challenge and delivered something good, every single one of them. We had a blast laughing.

* * *

Col's Note: The next morning my mother called to say she was watching coverage of the 50th anniversary of the assassination of President John F. Kennedy and that his presidential motorcade did indeed run through South Troy, right past our house on High Street, on September 29, 1960. "So you were just about two years old," she said. "I remember I got you dressed before I left to work. Your Papa (my grandfather Mark Murtagh) waited on the side of the road with you perched up on his shoulders so that you could wave when the President went by."

"I think I remember the President reached out and touched my hand," I said.

"Then that's probably right," Mom said.

* * * * *

Week 50, November 15, 2013

The Way God Works – You Can't Even Imagine

Three times this week I had to call Mom and cancel our book meeting date as I was working in full-steam ahead mode trying to set up launch events for my new book FIREFLIES, next-year teaching gigs, writing workshops, school visits, library programs, anything that will result in income for 2014, all the while wishing and hoping for good news about a contract for a new Willa book.

Here it was Friday and I had to call Mom yet again to say I couldn't meet at Jose Malone's restaurant as planned, but could she "just please come here for lunch?"

Mom still doesn't feel comfortable driving solo, so my wonderful son Dylan kindly offered to go pick her up. I only had ten minutes max to write my "good piece" before they arrived. Just as I started writing, the phone rang.

It was Rana D'Orio, my Little Pickle publisher.

"I have bad news," she said. The pub date for our *FIREFLIES: A Writer's Notebook* had been pushed out from Jan 20, 2014 to June 2014. This was a problem for me as I had just set up several spring school visits focused around this book.

Rana and I talked it through. There were a lot of good reasons why summer would be a better time to launch this title.

We discussed our first book, *BIG,* which came out in 2012. Rana just sold the rights for a Korean version and hoped to soon land a contract with Germany.

We talked about our families.

We talked about Thanksgiving.

I heard Mom and Dylan in the kitchen. I still hadn't written anything and I was starving, not having eaten since early this morning.

"Now let's talk about Willa," Rana said.

My mind swung back to full attention. *Please let this be good news.*

"I like Willa," Rana said.

She had read the first and sixth of the Willa books, then had her team read them and asked for their feedback, requested sales track records from my agent, had conversations with Ingram's (distributor) and other key people in the industry.

Here it comes....the "and I'm sorry, but..."

"I've done my due diligence," Rana said, "and I've put Willa in my 2014-15 financial plan."

I burst into tears. "Oh my gosh, Rana," I managed to say. "Thank you. You have no idea what this means to me..."

When I came out of my office, I shared the news with two of the most special people in my life. Dylan came forward and wrapped me in one of his quintessentially loving hugs. "I'm so happy for you, Mom. You've worked so hard. You deserve this."

My mother was overjoyed. "Oh, Col," she said. "That's wonderful."

I warmed up a can of soup, sliced a red grapefruit, all the while crying grateful tears. I have desperately missed writing about Willa. Finally, I will get the chance.

And this gift came when I least expected it. The way God works.

* * *

After lunch, Mom read:

psm, 11-15-13

You Can't Even Imagine

I've been doing this for almost a year now, this writing every week. Trying to think of something to say, and write, and read that's positive and worth saying, writing, and reading. And guess what? I only know that I haven't got the foggiest notion of where I am. Truth is, when I do finally get there – when I'm finally done -- I'll be done. Done done.

Well part of me is still this nice Catholic girl, and what I learned from early Catholic teachers is the same as what countless seekers of many faiths or no faith have learned. I'll say it like this: Whatever you've learned up to this point may not be the answer you've been looking for but I can tell you one thing – it's taught you that you can and must go back to Go and start over. Not because anything's wrong with what you've learned, but because every learning has brought you closer to understanding this: the learning is in fact the lesson.

Before I get off on some wordy tangent I want you to know that I'm currently reading two books cover to cover and that takes patience and fortitude. One is *Super Brain* co-authored by Deepak Chopra and Rudolph Tanz. And it takes me a long time to read smart so even though I'm on the last few chapters, it may be a week or a month or two days before I can say The End. The other book is *Many Lives Many Masters* by Brian Weiss. All these guys are renowned experts in their fields so I'm comfortable taking this reading time and I would certainly recommend them to any friend or foe. Again I thank Oprah because I found these books watching her priceless OWN network.

I hear the little gremlins in my brain bugging me, "What's your point, Peggy?" And my point is you just can't imagine. My scripture tidbits help me here again: "Eye has not seen, ear has not heard, nor has it entered into the mind of man (woman) what God has in store..."

Super Brain is today's latest research on the spiritual mind/body connection and how my brain is working its miracles right this minute. In *Many Lives, Many Masters* I'm introduced to past-life therapy. Where do we go when our human physical journey comes to an end? Dr. Weiss went from non-believing to believing, i.e., we've been here before and we'll be here again. (I don't know where I was in 1988 when this book was becoming 'a timeless classic' on the New York Times bestseller list. I was probably having a heart attack, or having open heart surgery, feeling despair at either Four Winds in Saratoga or the psych ward at Samaritan Hospital.)

My psychotherapist, another smart and gifted doctor I trust tells me this writing with Coleen has been very positive, healing and therapeutic for me. A gift from my daughter. My faith remains my gift. And I know the words "Eye has not seen..." keep coming true for me. I can't even imagine what tomorrow will bring. Life is more than good; it's a miracle very worth living.

* * * * *

Week 51, November 20, 2013

Glowing With Good – Four Score and Seven

We had lunch at Beirut Restaurant on River Street, "A taste of Lebanon in downtown Troy." The charismatically charming owner, Elias G. Haj Nasr, won an autographed copy of my book, *BIG*, at the Troy 100 Forum earlier this week and as we chatted afterwards, he said: "You must come to my restaurant!"

"I'll bring my Mom this week," I promised.

Elias welcomed us like we were royalty and could not have been more gracious, smiling and lighting up the room with good energy, definitely a "PEP."

Handing us menus he said, "Thank you, thank you."

Taking our drink orders he said, "Thank you, thank you."

He described with great pride how his wife/partner Hala prepares their hummus and baba ghanoush, falafel, tabouli and stuffed grape leaves. "Thank you, thank you."

"What a wonderful man," my mother said.

"He's absolutely full of joy," I said. "That is so nice to see."

Elias shared his story of coming to America in need of work, leaving a respected position as an architect and artist. He showed us some of his paintings. He bragged about his children and grandchildren. The food was superb.

After we placed our dessert order, Mom slid a small white bag with a yellow ribbon across the table to me. "Happy birthday, Col."

There was a notecard with a purple ink stamp of a lady and this quote:

The two most beautiful words in the
English language are "check enclosed."

—Dorothy Parker

"That's our girl," I said, and we laughed.

Inside the bag were two presents.

One, a poem Mom had written for me, typed on a simple white piece of paper, folded into quarters. I smoothed it out and read it silently, slowly savoring each word.

Go Girl Go
Happy Birthday to Col
11-21-13

There she goes
My go girl go
Got me writing
Who could know

She keeps running
Toward her dreams
Always bringing
Me it seems

Not just me but everyone
Every day
Til day is done

Coleen always says thank you
Then, what comes next
Well gratitude
completes her text

She seems to say
And means it too
I want this to be
Good for you

So Good for you
My go girl go
I so want you to always know
You've been a dream come true for me

The simple words keep rolling out
And I should know
Without a doubt
my thanks are just
and so I shout

You helped me stop crying
So I could keep trying
Because you care

You go girl go
And I'll be there

"This is so beautiful, Mom," I said, wiping mascara from my cheeks. Elias had observed what was going on and respectfully gave us our space. "Thank you so much."

"Thank *you*, sweet girl. There's something more." Mom nodded toward the bag.

A simple white envelope.

From: Mom
To: Coleen
Happy Belated
But So Beloved
Birthday

I unsealed the envelope.

Inside was a check made out to me.

The amount made me gasp and burst into tears again. I shook my head in disbelief. "Mom.... are you sure?"

"Oh my dear girl. You deserve this and so much more."

"We couldn't have gotten Camp Russell without you, Col," she said.

"But Mom," I said. "Are you sure you can do this?"

"Absolutely sure."

Elias served us our Baklava and coffees, smiling, "thank you, thank you."

It was a perfect birthday party and perfect lead in to what I had written to share:

cmp, 11-20-13

Glowing With Good

I know it sounds crazy to say this, but I feel like I am glowing with good.

Lit from within, light all around me, each day brings some new awareness... connection... opportunity for work that feels like "right work." Happy, joy-filled, grateful, I am bursting with energy and excitement for living, looking forward to several new books I want to write, classes I want to teach, new ways I want to help make life better for the children of Troy, especially the poor and disenfranchised.

I want to make my fledgling program TREAT (Troy Reads Every August Together) a really BIG event next summer. At Monday night's Troy 100 Forum—a gathering of leaders wanting to move Troy forward, the brainchild of my brilliantly glowing friend, Fred Miller--I asked for help to make this happen. The Mayor of Troy, Lou Rosamilia, was among the many to offer help. I also announced my intention to build Little Free Libraries in Troy locations where children don't have easy access to the library or money to buy books, and several people signed up to assist with this as well.

Yesterday I told my friend, Lisa Lewis, Editor of *The Record* that I want to write a weekly column for the paper. We're meeting soon to discuss that possibility.

For years I've been telling my friends and family that I want to "do something really big for the girls of Troy some day" and this morning out running I got clear about starting a foundation to bring my Read*Write*Roar*Return program on the road. I also want to award a college scholarship to "One Kid from Troy" each year.

At a Rensselaer County Chamber of Commerce breakfast event yesterday – A College Presidents Roundtable hosted by my amazing friend and mentor Wally Altes – I learned a full year at HVCC is only $3, 900. It struck me that I could easily raise that money just by offering parties and dinners at my own home and invite relatives, friends, and fans to pitch in. I have lots of connections, circles of support.

Last Saturday I attended the Veg Fest, celebration of vegetarian/vegan/healthy lifestyles with my glowing goddaughter Lauren and after soaking in much knowledge, I decided that I am going green. I've been moving toward it for years but now am clear the time is right. I am on fire, inspired, infused with spirit and clarity. Happy.

I was born to teach and write. These are my talents. Each morning I ask God to lead me, tell me how to *use my life* for good. And then I try to listen. Looking back now, last fall when my fiction writing kept hitting one roadblock after another and I was scared to death about paying bills, perhaps that was God's way of directing me toward a new path, toward more teaching and new forms of writing... opening my schedule and redirecting my creative energy and talent to this book with my Mom. If I had been in the "cave mode" I so crave when writing fiction, I never could have been fully present to this miracle we've been moving through.

God is good and glowing in me.

⁂

"Perfect," my mother said. Then she shared her piece:

psm, 11-20-13

Four Score and Seven

The written word holds new strength and meaning for me. For most of the last year I've written my own words every week, making an effort with my daughter Coleen to say something positive. I consider myself a word person.

Last night I watched on PBS a documentary about The Gettysburg Address. So what did I learn that I thought I already knew?

In 1863, President Abraham Lincoln you might say had written the book on stress and depression. He carried an almost unbearable guilt over the Civil War and the countless lives that had been sacrificed both in the North and the South. The Emancipation Proclamation, more than one of those definitions and dates we had to learn as school kids, was in fact a reality that almost tore our nation apart. Lincoln couldn't know it at the time, but his brief words dedicating the Gettysburg cemetery to more than 50,000 men who had died in battle would become immortal: copied, published, read and re-read. I know I had to learn the address back in my early school time, no different than countless students in the decades before and the decades to follow.

If you want to talk about the power of the written word, the Gettysburg Address fits the bill. Lincoln's brief remarks were by no means the star billing that day. A renowned speaker, the best orator of his day (whose name escapes me), preceded Lincoln and talked for two hours. This length of time was not unusual; this was before electronic media and the people wanted to listen and hear what the great voices had to say. The president's few short remarks may have seemed almost anti-climatic. They were meant to honor the dead and bless the hallowed ground.

I was surprised to learn, although I must have heard it, that Lincoln's words at Gettysburg are among the briefest uttered by any president before or since. The count of the words that would become immortal totaled 272; just ten sentences. Although spoken with a great reverence and dignity, his words lasted just three minutes. Think about it.

The tall man with the sad face spoke words reminding us that these dead should *not have died in vain*; and that our nation was *conceived in liberty and dedicated to the proposition that all men are created equal.*

Now it's 2013 and the power of the written word still holds my respect. Its value offers me a new dimension. Not that I'm hearing these words considered a masterpiece of great oratory for the first time. Rather, that I can remember a great man, simple and humble and broken over the unspeakable carnage of the battlefield, who gave us hope *that these dead shall not have died in vain*, and that this *this nation of the people, by the people and for the people shall not perish...* and, I think, is worth finding a way of peace.

* * * * *

Week 52, Part 1, November 26, 2013

Gratitude for Cousins

I was so crazy busy this week with work and preparations for Thanksgiving that I completely forgot Mom and I were supposed to meet at Lo Porto's restaurant downtown for our final session. Me, who writes down everything, and checks calendars constantly. I blame it on denial. I have loved this experience so much and don't want to see it end. Perhaps my subconscious, my Spirit, is saying "this work isn't over yet."

Here is the piece Mom was going to read at Lo Porto's:

psm, 11-26-13

Gratitude for Cousins

I needed time to pray and meditate this morning. I always know what I'm missing, what I haven't done yet and too rarely remember what I have right now as I live and breathe. That's when gratitude is remembered.

Gratitude right now has me remembering cousins. Spain cousins because I'm part of an old Irish Catholic family of Spains that have been in Troy for generations. For me cousin is spiritual -- makes me think of Jesus and his cousins (and who knows whether they were His brothers or cousins; both I believe while the biblical scholars are still trying to get that straight along with everything else.

This past week I was with cousins at a very meaningful, respectful reception to honor my Cousin Ed. Honorable fits him perfectly because more than 'His Honor' on the bench, Ed is an honorable man in every way and has been throughout his life. This was a big gala attended by every judge, more judges than I've ever seen in one place at one time, all there to honor Ed at his retirement after nearly fifty years as a judge, all in our home town, moving up the judgeship journey starting as Troy police court judge right up to his current seat at the top of New York State juris prudence.

My point is that among the throng of judges and other professionals, not the least of which was our Troy mayor , all honored guests, Ed wanted his family there. And of course cousins are part of what Ed means by family. There I was sitting at a table of Spain cousins. It brought me back to my growing up time (and that's a nice thing to happen when you're 75 going on 76). Ed's brother, my Cousin Dan, was there remembering me (Dan's brilliant special mind never forgets a name or a face). I recalled taking Dan in the stroller when I was about 14 and Dan maybe 2 or 3 and I was trusted to take Dan for an outing over to Beman Park from the house at 2301 Burdett Ave. It was always referred to as "the house," meaning that's where all the Spain's, including my fathe,r were raised and where my Aunt Joe and Uncle Jack , my dad's brother, still lived with their large family.

The cousin heartfelt remembrance there at Franklin Plaza brought me together with many cousins, like Cousin Ned, now 80 and looking fit and handsome with a lady friend, he the son of my own Uncle Ned, another of my father's brothers.

Cousin Mary was there with her husband Jeff and they sat across the table from me. In our cousin circle, she sat next to Dan and his caretaker (Dan is always accompanied by an aide from his group home in Troy.) Mimi, my youngest loving sister who drove me, sat next to me on my right, and on my left another cousin, my brother Jim, looking handsome and almost fit recovering as he is from malignant tumors, with his beautiful wife Sue who has and is attending to his every need.

My point is there were dozens of cousins that took me back to a family time when I was young and fragile but growing strong guided by my cousin Ed's mother who was my godmother, my Aunt Jo. She was the saving angel in my growing up time and she took care of her eight children, Joseph, Edward, Johnny, Danny, Mary, Michael, Francis and Anthony, as well as her husband's (Uncle Jack's) family: Aunt Marie, Uncle Walter and later my Aunt Margaret (who I'm named after) -- all Spain's, all my aunts, uncles and cousins.

A cousin's table at the Franklin Plaza gala was my honorable Cousin Ed's gift of recognition and remembrance. Cousins are family. Also, as well as I felt the spirit of his mother and father, my Aunt Jo and Uncle Jack, I remembered that there was a ninth child, little Ann, who died after a difficult birth. (Maybe it's because I know the pain of losing a newborn child, I can't think of all those eight cousins without a thought for a ninth cousin, little Ann.)

Cousins are a treasure, for which I have an everlasting gratitude.

* * * * *

Week 52, Part 2, November 30, 2013

Aunt Mary's Meatballs – Thanksgiving

The plan was for me to pick up my mother at 4:45pm for a 5:00 dinner reservation and final "good session" over dinner at LoPorto's, followed by *An Nollaig: An Irish Christmas with Eileen Ivers* at the Troy Music Hall. I had purchased tickets for us thinking this would be a fitting celebration for our year long work together.

At 4:30 p.m. I was still typing my final entry, not showered or dressed. I rushed out to the kitchen and said, "Columbus, I need you please to do two things for me: 1) go pick up my Mom and bring her here, and 2) call LoPorto's and switch my reservation to 5:30.

"Got it, Luv," he said.

Later, down in the driveway as Columbus escorted my Mom into the front seat of my car, I told Columbus how grateful I was. "Thanks so much, Babe. You made our first session possible – remember how you came home and plowed out the driveway so I could get to my Mom's house – and now you made our last meeting happen."

"Have a good time with your Mom, Luv."

"I love you," I said.

"I love you more."

At the restaurant, I noticed my mother had taken extra special care with her clothes and jewelry and hair. "You look beautiful, Mom," I said, suggesting we switch seats so that she faced the room, secretly hoping that one of those well-dressed older gentlemen at the bar would see this gorgeous silver haired lady and come speak to her.

Mom read first:

Aunt Mary's Meatballs

I called Mary Fox today and it was a blessed reunion between two old aunts who are related by marriage but have been separated for too many years. Coleen wanted Aunt Mary's Swedish meatball recipe to be part of a possible "favorite recipes" section in our book and had been urging me for weeks to call Aunt Mary.

Every year at the large family gathering that included grab bags, games, music, dancing, storytelling, family sharing, hosted by Col and Tony, we all brought a dish or dessert for the informal pot luck which was anything but informal -- this was a holiday feast. Aunt Mary's Swedish Meatballs were everybody's favorite and took first prize every year when we all voted for the best dish.

When I talked to Mary today she confided, expressing her long held guilt, that these were her secret meatballs, not made from scratch at all but purchased frozen from BJ's which she thawed at home and combined with what I call her magic sauce. Being the good Catholic girl of my generation, Mary had carried her meatball guilt for 20 some years and she was finally able to make her 'Confession' to me. She was so happy to be able to finally do that. Being a good old Catholic girl myself, I assured Mary she had nothing to feel guilty about and should feel nothing but joy knowing that she had brought so much to so many for all those Christmas celebration times.

Here's what Mary shared with me today. Any of us who've prepared something special for a special occasion will appreciate what Mary made happen for us.

One large bag (100?) frozen Swedish meatballs (she got them at BJs)

2 cans Campbell's mushroom gravy soup.

One pkg. Lipton's dry onion soup dip mix

At home, defrost meatballs spread out in heated oven on deep cookie sheet.

When thawed (Mary always tasted one because they're already cooked) combine soup and onion mix and pour over the meatballs in a large oven safe bowl. Stir to coat all the meatballs. Return to oven and cook until well heated.

Mary served them in a large stainless steel bowl so use whatever they'll fit into.

* * *

"Oh, Mom," I said, as we laughed together. "B.J.s? Really? That's priceless. How is Aunt Mary?" Mom filled me in. "I miss seeing her," I said. "I love her."

The marinara sauce on my Eggplant Parmesan was the best I've ever had. Mom said her scallops were "delicious." I read this:

cmp, 11-29-13

THANKSGIVING

Yesterday was my happiest Thanksgiving Day ever.

I kept the food thing simple... Betty Crocker 101...with "everybody please bring something." Family members happily signed up for appetizers, pies and beverages.

My beautiful and unbelievably generous sister-in-law Colleen, niece Lauren and nephew Brendan, came the day before and for three blessed hours helped peel potatoes, make stuffing, do place cards, etc. I could not have pulled it off without them.

Columbus completed a mile long "honey do" list with nary a single complaint.

Dylan and Connor came with bags of groceries the night before. Dylan made a kick-ass appetizer involving chicken, chipotle, avocado and *phyllo*... yes, phyllo. Connor downloaded a list of songs I love into a "Thanksgiving" playlist. Such a gift.

On Thanksgiving morning, Connor, Lauren, Columbus and I ran the Turkey Trot in downtown Troy. Lauren's parents, Kevin and Colleen, cheered us on from the halfway point in front of the Ale House on River Street. It was freezing, only 25 degrees out, but exhilarating and *so much fun*!!!

Everyone arrived for appetizers at 1:00 pm. Mom with her classic and much loved chicken liver pate; beautiful brother Jerry from Brooklyn with the ingredients to whip up award-winning vegan stuffed mushrooms and to-die-for hot chocolate; my gorgeous sister, Nor, brother-in-law Michael, dear nephews Ryan and Jack, with not one, but two homemade apple pies, a huge container of Nor's special Thanksgiving stuffing (requested by my son Dylan), a case of good wine (I love my brother-in-law!) and a big basket full of belated birthday presents for me (I love my, sister!) Kev, Coll, Lauren, and dear nephews Liam and Brendan brought a gluten-free pumpkin pie and vegan pumpkin pie and oh-my-gosh amazing gluten-free chocolate chip cookies and beer and soda. Chris arrived with bags of potato chips and our family's favorite Heluva onion dip.

While the boys and men all watched football in the living room or played ping pong/Rock Band/video games downstairs...Mom, Nor, Coll, Lauren and I... three generations of great girls... all moved about my tiny kitchen working to get everything ready while chatting and singing along to the playlist Connor had made...and I thought I might explode I was so grateful, and so very very happy.

And then there we all were... 16 of the people I love most in the world...all together in *my house*...around a long rectangle (my kitchen table with two add-on folding tables) adorned with beautiful gold and brown linens that Columbus had brought home from Morgan Linen, festooned with bouquets of red and gold bittersweet and milkweed pods (that I had clipped during a run around the Frear Park Golf course), Dollar Store frames with sixteen of my favorite inspirational quotes as place markers, and votive candles, lots of them. I asked each person to say something, "Say Anything" a shout out to Nor's improv company, and each person said something she or he was grateful for. Then my mother said her Spanish prayer that we have all come to expect at the start of any family meal and we began to eat.

I smiled at Columbus and reached to clutch his hand under the table.

Thank you, God. Thank you.

* * *

"Oh that's just perfect, Col," my mother said.

* * * * *

December 6, 2013

Peg and Col's Thoughts Moving Forward

We met for tea at my house at 3:00 pm. Mom read this:

psm, 12-6-13

Peg Moving Forward

I followed my daughter Coleen's lead this year. But she would be the first to acknowledge that whatever I have written has been me writing; no one else. This 12 month effort rests in my heart as one of the real life miracles that was given to me by a loving God whom I too often forget to remember. I never quite find the words to express what I want to express; a living breathing sacrament has come over me.

Coleen wanted us as mother and daughter to share our positive stories and there were weeks- many weeks - when this effort seemed beyond my ability. But I looked at a blank page week after week and the guidance of Holy Spirit spoke to me and moved my fingers and filled the emptiness with fullness.

So what will I do now to nurture this inspiration?

Praying and writing more of my story seems the only way to go.

Over the years there have been times when I would tell my story in bits and pieces -- sometimes in the classroom or alone or just sharing with friends. Because so many work-years were spent serving an executive above me, the thought came to me years ago: someday I'll call my autobiography "Call My Secretary." Of course that means I tried to learn to support myself as I had been paid to support the bosses above me. Maybe that title will stick; or maybe something else will speak to my inner Peggy; we'll see.

It just came to me – maybe I'll call my next writing Peggy's Poems or Peggy's Prose and Poetry. There's something waiting to be spoken and the Holy Spirit will speak to me. I just have to pay attention and listen and ready-or-not here it will come.

To be continued.

⁂

"Oh Mom, that's wonderful!" I was clapping. "I'm so glad you are finally going to write your life story! You've always wanted to do that. It will be *amazing*."

My mother sipped her tea. There was a calm confidence about her.

"I think you should title it Call My Secretary," I said, "unless our book hits the best-seller list and your name becomes a household word like Oprah or Ellen…then definitely go with Peggy's Prose and Poetry."

Mom cracked up.

"No seriously, Mom," I said. "I dreamt we were on the "Today" show. Matt Lauer read aloud something you'd written then shook his head respectfully and said, "Peggy, that's powerful."

Mom laughed. "If you say so."

Then I shared this:

cmp, 12-6-13

Col's Thoughts Moving Forward

When I got that firefly idea --"*Mom and I should write a book together*" jogging on Thanksgiving morning 2012, I was excited about how this project might help *her*.

What I didn't know was just how good it would be for *me*.

This was a life-changing, transformative year. When I look back to where I was emotionally, physically, financially....all that I anguished over that winter....and how new shoots grew in the spring... only to be dragged down by a dark "muck and muddle" summer...then up again and onward in autumn when *everything* in my life seemed basked in a golden light...to a full circle December, winter again, and an inner peace I can only call holy...*this is what happy is.*

Mom and I kept our promise. For one whole year, we wrote ourselves forward. Now, what next?

I want to make a new commitment to meeting weekly with Mom, beginning in January. I want to finish the book "on writing" I've been working on for years. Hopefully Mom will finally write her memoir. We could meet for lunch at a Troy restaurant, a booth by the window when possible, and each bring a new chapter to read.

What say you, Mom? Are you up for a new challenge?

* * *

I stared across the table at her. "What do you think, Mom? You're going to need a sequel, you know. When people read your first book, they're going to want more."

My mother laughed.

Long silence. That's my Mom. No one rushes her.

"Okay," she said finally in a soft voice. Then loudly, smiling: "Yes."

"Hooray!" I shouted, clapping, and we laughed.

I noticed the time and stood to clear our tea mugs. Columbus was coming home soon. We were going to get our Christmas tree.

Mom took a manila envelope out of her bag. "I had a good meeting with Ellen McNulty (funeral director) on Monday," she said, unfolding a document. "Ellen said preplanning one's funeral is one of the kindest gifts a parent can give their children."

Oh boy. I wasn't expecting this. I sat back down and listened with loving attention as my mother shared specifics on the coffin she had chosen ("one of the least expensive"), and the encasement ("the least expensive"), details about calling hours, etc. She was surprised at how expensive obituary notices would be. "I told Ellen to just put a write up in the *Troy Record*. The *Times Union* costs too much."

"Oh no, Mom," I said. "I'll make sure you have a really big write up in both."

"Ellen offered me a burial plot she has up in St. Peter's Cemetery," Mom said.

"That was so nice of her," I said. St. Peter's is a small, old Catholic cemetery across the street from the famous Oakwood Cemetery where Uncle Sam and Emma Willard, among other American notables, are buried.

"I jog through St. Peter's sometimes," I said, swallowing a lump in my throat as I imagined a future day jogging past my mother's memorial marker (a park bench with perennial flowers) waving, smiling, blowing a kiss. *I love you, Mom. I love you.*

When my mother was finished, I thanked her for sharing this with me. "We won't need this for a very long time, Mom, but I am grateful you did this."

"I feel relieved," she said, smiling.

⁂ ⁂ ⁂ ⁂ ⁂

December 13, 2013

Celebrating an Ending and a Beginning

Mom and I went to see the Theatre Institute at Sage's production of *The Secret Garden*. It was beautiful, moving and inspirational.

After, we drove to Moscatiello's on Rte 4 for lunch. Yesterday I brought some things to be tailored at the owner's wife, Maria's, Sewing Center, nearby the restaurant and when I told Maria and her daughters (they all sew together...super women... I love them) about what my mother and I were writing, it dawned on me that we just had to include Moscatiello's in the book and so here we were.

The food was delicious; the atmosphere, festive. We talked about Christmas. Mom was flying to Charlotte, NC to spend two weeks with my brother Michael and Donnie. I was sad to think this was the first Christmas I wouldn't see my mother, but so happy for my brother to have this time with her.

We made plans to do a holiday dinner at my house in January.

I shared how the offer on the Cape house had fallen through and how worried I was about paying that mortgage. "My realtor planted another St. Joseph statue for good luck," I said, "and she's got one on her desk, too. St. Joe needs to step up his game."

Mom laughed. "It will sell in the spring," she said confidently.

We shared a piece of chocolate-raspberry cake for dessert.

"I made a list of Troy restaurants we haven't hit yet," I said, "there's at least 40."

Mom laughed, shook her head and rolled her eyes.

"We're still going to keep meeting, right Mom?"

"Yes,"

"Then let's set a date to start," I said.

We took out our calendars.

"How about Monday, January 6th," I suggested.

"Okay."

"Lunch or dinner?"

"Let's do dinner."

"How about 5pm?"

"Okay."

And so, *hooray*, we'll soon be off again, embarking on a new adventure -- not together, but side by side, not knowing for sure where the writing will lead us, but knowing it will be right.

The End

THA
CONWAY COURT
APARTMENTS
TROY HOUSING AUTHO

Sweet Sues
A Treatery

Peg and Col's "Pix List" of Recommended Inspirational Books

Alcott, Louisa May, *Little Women*

Albom, Mitch, *Tuesdays with Morrie*

Anderson, Joan, *A Year by the Sea*

Anderson, Joan, *The Second Journey, The Road Back to Yourself*

Angelou, Maya, *I Know Why the Caged Bird Sings*

Applegate, Katherine, *The One and Only Ivan*

Bell, Rob, *What We Talk About When We Talk About God*

Berg, Elizabeth, *Escaping Into the Open, The Art of Writing True*

Borysenko, Joan, *A Woman's Journey to God*

Borysenko, Joan, *Pocketful of Miracles*

Breathnach, Sarah Ban, *Simple Abundance*

Bourgeois, Roy M.M., *My Journey from Silence to Solidarity*

Brown, Brene`, *Daring Greatly*

Callan, James Brady, *Pioneer Priest*

Cameron, Diane, *Looking for Signs*

Cameron, Julia, *The Artist's Way: A Spiritual Path to Higher Creativity*

Campbell, Joseph, *The Power of Myth*

Capote, Truman, *A Christmas Memory*

Chittister, Joan, *Monastery of the Heart* (Peg's note: "and anything else by her")

Chodron, Pema, *Awakening Loving-Kindness*

Chodron, Pema, *The Pocket Pema Chodron*

Chopra, Deepak, *Super Brain*

Collins, Billy, *Aimless Love*

Dickens, Charles, *A Christmas Carol*

Dillard, Annie, *The Writing Life*

Gilbert, Elizabeth, *Eat, Pray, Love*

Goldberg, Natalie, *Writing Down the Bones*

Goldberg, Natalie, *Wild Mind: Living the Writer's Life*
Greenway, Kate, *Language of Flowers*
Hanh, Thich Nhat, *The Miracle of Mindfulness*
Hesse, Herman, *Siddhartha*
Jamison, Kaleel, *The Nibble Theory and the Kernel of Power*
Johnson, Damone Paul, *A Life Worth Rebuilding*
Joyce, Rachel, *The Unlikely Pilgrimage of Harold Fry*
Julian of Norwich, *Revelations of Divine Love*
Katz, Judith H. and Frederick A. Miller, *Be BIG*
Kennedy, Caroline, *The Best-Loved Poems of Jacqueline Kennedy Onassis*
Kennedy, Caroline, *Poems to Learn by Heart*
Kenison, Katrina, *Magical Journey*
King, Stephen, *On Writing*
Lamott, Anne, *Bird by Bird: Some Instructions on Writing and Life*
Lamott, Anne, *Stitches: A Handbook on Meaning, Hope and Repair*
Lesser, Elizabeth, *Broken Open*
Lindbergh, Ann Morrow, *Gift from the Sea*
McCourt, Frank, *Angela's Ashes*
Mandela, Nelson, *2010 Book of Letters*
Mandela, Nelson, *Long Walk to Freedom*
May, Rollo, *The Courage to Create*
May, Rollo, *A Course in Miracles*
Merton, Thomas, *Daily Meditations*
Merton, Thomas, *The Pocket Thomas Merton*
Mitchell, Stephen, *Tao Te Ching, A New English Version*
Montgomery, L.M., *Anne of Green Gables*
Moore, Thomas, *Care of the Soul*
Morrison, Toni, *Song of Solomon*
Northrup, M.D., Christine, *Women's Wisdom, A Calendar to Use Year After Year*
O'Connor, Flannery, *A Prayer Journal*

Oliver, Mary, *New and Selected Poems, Volumes 1 and 2*

Paterson, Katherine, *Giving Thanks: Poems, Prayers, and Praise Songs of Thanksgiving*

Quindlen, Anna, *Lots of Candles, Plenty of Cake*

Reynolds, Sil & Eliza, *MOTHERING & DAUGHTERING*

Roach, Margaret, *The Backyard Parables*

Roach Smith, Marion, *The Memoir Project*

Roberts, Cokie, *We Are Our Mother's Daughters*

Ruiz, Don Miguel, *The Four Agreements*

Sarton, May, *Journal of a Solitude*

Smith, Betty, *A Tree Grows in Brooklyn*

Sotomayor, Sonia, *My Beloved World*

Thoreau, Henry David, *Walden*

Upjohn, Sheila, *Daily Readings from Julian of Norwich*

Vanzant, Iyanla, *Peace from Broken Pieces*

Voskamp, Ann, *One Thousand Gifts: A Dare to Live Fully Right Where You Are*

Walker, Alice, *In Search of Our Mothers' Gardens*

Walker, Alice, *The Color Purple*

Willard, Nancy, *The Left-Handed Story: Writing and the Writer's Life*

Wilder, Thornton, *Our Town*

Yousafzai, Malala with Christina Lamb, *I Am Malala*

Peg's Acknowledgements:

I have neither the memory or emotional or physical strength to name here all the scores upon scores of people whose presence in my life have made this work possible. My heartfelt thanks to each of you; with special acknowledgement to my children: Coleen, Mark, Michael, Noreen, Joseph, Jerry, Dan and Kevin (6 on earth and 2 in heaven); my brothers and sisters: Janie, Virginia, Mimi, Charley, Jim and my half-sister Cindy; my precious grandchildren: Chris, Connor, Dylan, Ryan, Jack, Liam, Lauren and Brendan; my daughters-in-love: Colleen McNulty Murtagh, Lianne Terrio and Donnie Reznek; soul sisters and brothers past and present, including: Mary Jane Smith, Terry Page, Alice and Bill McLoughlin, Joanne Coyle, Martha Walsh, Sisters Rita Shawn and Maria Cokely, Tracy Neitzel, Paul Delio, Steve Banbury, Mary Theresa Streck, Petra Hahn, Shenise Foskey, Caroline Smith, Maureen Noonan, Stanley Hadsell, Rita Watson, Sally Brennan, Phyllis Fobare, Joannie Costa, Barb Cassella, Tom and Carol DeLeo, and Jean Pelerin; the professional caregivers without whom I could not have done positive work this year including: Drs Musto, Padi, VanDyne, Atalay, Sue Brownell, Morris and Echt; and spiritual travelers past and present: Jay Murnane, Tom Phelan, Randy Paterson, Brian O'Shaughnessy, Rich Broderick, and Howard Hubbard.

It's true that naming all the souls who have touched my heart this year is not possible; please know that you are in my heart.

Gratefully,

Peg

Col's Acknowledgements:

With sincere gratitude to my three sons, my suns, Dylan, Connor, and Christopher Paratore, who bless me with their love and belief in me; to Columbus Buish, who cheers me on daily and makes me so happy; to my wonderful family: Noreen, Michael, Ryan and Jack Mahoney; Jerry Murtagh; Colleen, Kevin, Liam, Lauren and Brendan Murtagh; Michael Murtagh and Donnie Reznek; Danny Murtagh and Lianne Terrio; and to all of my supportive relatives and many circles of friends, especially those who offered encouraging sparks for this particular book: Stanley Hadsell, Susan Novotny, Pauline Kamen Miller, Fred Miller, Corey Jamison, Kathy Johnson, Rachel King, Joanne Skerrit, Peter Marino, Kathleen Elken, Ellen Laird, Robyn Ryan, Eric Luper, Kyra Teis, Marion Roach Smith, Lisa Lewis, Carol Chittenden, Cynthia O'Brien, Jamie Holmes, my students at The Arts Center of the Capital Region, and with extra special thanks to publishing world friends Barb Burg and Nan Gatewood Satter for wise early advice and encouragement, and to writer friends extraordinaire, Ellen Laird and Kathleen Elken, for reading through the final manuscript and helping us over the finish line.

I am so grateful to have you in my life.

With much love,

Col

Writing Sparks & Conversation Starters

Perhaps some of the topics we considered will serve as sparks for your writing or conversation starters for a book club, class, workshop, retreat, or other group gathering.

- favorite poets ~ poems
- journal writing
- music
- wise advice
- community service
- grandchildren/children
- meditation
- rainbows
- holidays after divorce or other major life loss
- "your" parks
- faith
- powerful letters you have written or received
- your all-time favorite books
- inspirational quotes
- spiritual teachers
- someone who's been like a mother or father to you
- firefly ideas
- cherished birthday memories
- positive energy people in your life
- happy experiences with the arts
- your hometown
- comfort foods
- favorite recipes

- who has loved you unconditionally?
- kismet moments in your life
- moving from darkness to light
- your "right work"
- favorite bookstores
- beloved pets
- important women in your life
- neighbors/neighborhoods
- organized religion: pro's and con's
- your mother's dream
- angels
- flowers ~ gardens
- someone you've done business with for years
- what would you say to Oprah or other famous person who has greatly inspired you?
- a time when you felt forsaken
- losing a place you love
- Spring
- signs
- teachers you will never forget
- have you ever felt the spiritual presence of a deceased loved one?
- birds
- interesting family history stories
- exercise
- a spot/place in nature that holds special meaning for you
- moving through loss
- a book that greatly inspired you/books you read again and again
- your mother
- your father
- a time when one person made all the difference

- friends who are like sisters or brothers
- the ocean
- lost and found
- a bridge that holds special meaning for you
- Mother Earth
- Father's Day
- someone who was kind to you as a child
- freedom
- labor
- the will to live
- your dream partner
- achieving peace
- your bucket list
- road trips
- cursive writing
- diets
- a plan that would be helpful for you to write
- recent setbacks in your life
- a talisman/superstition that worked for you
- matchmaking
- an "extreme dreamer" you admire
- an unexpected invitation
- what did you want to be when you grew up? ☺
- 9/11
- Autumn
- a childhood memory related to food
- the town/city you live in now
- big questions you have for a loved one
- walking
- dancing

- heaven
- smiling
- female spiritual leaders
- education
- anticipation
- Sunday mornings
- favorite weekend breakfast spot
- family traditions
- handwritten messages
- birthday cards
- sexual abuse
- remembering the forgotten
- a new direction
- baseball (or your favorite sport)
- Halloween
- voting
- laughter~humor~funny people
- meeting a president or other noted political leader
- a shocking gift
- the way God works
- happiness
- cousins
- the subconscious
- Spirit
- Thanksgiving
- is there a book you have always wanted to write?
- is there a new goal you'd like to set?
- is there someone you'd like to "write it right" with?

Your Pages